THE SHRINE OF
OUR LADY OF WALSINGHAM

THE SHRINE OF OUR LADY OF WALSINGHAM

BY

J. C. DICKINSON

*Fellow and Chaplain of Pembroke College,
Cambridge*

CAMBRIDGE
AT THE UNIVERSITY PRESS
1956

CAMBRIDGE UNIVERSITY PRESS
Cambridge, New York, Melbourne, Madrid, Cape Town,
Singapore, São Paulo, Delhi, Tokyo, Mexico City

Cambridge University Press
The Edinburgh Building, Cambridge CB2 8RU, UK

Published in the United States of America by
Cambridge University Press, New York

www.cambridge.org
Information on this title: www.cambridge.org/9780521240550

© Cambridge University Press 1956

This publication is in copyright. Subject to statutory exception
and to the provisions of relevant collective licensing agreements,
no reproduction of any part may take place without the written
permission of Cambridge University Press.

First published 1956
First paperback edition 2011

A catalogue record for this publication is available from the British Library

ISBN 978-0-521-24055-0 Paperback

Cambridge University Press has no responsibility for the persistence or
accuracy of URLs for external or third-party internet websites referred to in
this publication, and does not guarantee that any content on such websites is,
or will remain, accurate or appropriate.

To
GEORGE
and
MICHAEL

CONTENTS

List of Illustrations *page* ix
Preface xi
List of Abbreviations xii

PART I. HISTORICAL

I THE ORIGINS OF THE SHRINE 3
II THE PROGRESS OF PILGRIMAGE 24
III THE LAST DAYS 48

PART II. ARCHAEOLOGICAL

IV THE CHURCH AND CLOISTERS 71
V THE PLACES OF PILGRIMAGE 91
VI MISCELLANEA: SEALS, STATUE, BADGES, ETC. 108

Appendix I THE PYNSON BALLAD 124
Appendix II PRIORS OF WALSINGHAM 131
Appendix III CANONS OF WALSINGHAM 135
Appendix IV THE SLIPPER CHAPEL 141

Bibliographical Note 143
Index 145

LIST OF ILLUSTRATIONS

*The plates are at the end of the book,
between pp. 144 and 145*

Ground-plan of the priory   *between pp. 106 and 107*

PLATE 1   Walsingham Priory, from the engraving by Buck, 1738

PLATE 2   The East end of the church

PLATE 3   (a) The priory from the air; (b) St Laurence's chapel

PLATE 4   (a) The refectory; (b) the wells

PLATE 5   The undercroft

PLATE 6   Seals, etc.

  (a) First seal of Walsingham
  (b) Badge of Our Lady of Rocamadour
  (c) Later seal of Walsingham (obverse)
  (d) Later seal of Walsingham (reverse)

PLATE 7   Architectural details

  (a) Capital (c. 1180)
  (b) Twin capitals (c. 1240)
  (c) Gargoyle (c. 1400)
  (d) Stone panel (c. 1500)

LIST OF ILLUSTRATIONS

PLATE 8 Badges and ampulla

(a) B.M., 91/4–18/25   (b) London, Guildhall Museum, 8689

(c) and (e) B.M., Hugo Collection   (d) B.M., 60/9–7/3

The sources of these badges are: (a) London; (b) probably Thames; (c) London ? (d) River Somme, Picardy; (e) London (?).

PLATE 9 Badges and ampullae

(a) and (b) Mill Fleet, King's Lynn (now lost)

(c) and (d) King's Lynn Museum

(e) Present whereabouts and size unknown

(f), (g) and (h) King's Lynn Museum

(i) Oxford, Ashmolean Museum 1927/6409

The sources are: (c) and (d) Mill Fleet; (e) Fincham, Norfolk; (f),(g) and (h) Mill Fleet; (i) Icklingham, Suffolk.

PREFACE

THE following pages are a much amplified version of a lecture given to the Royal Archaeological Institute. Circumstances having prevented my attempting a definitive study of the priory of Walsingham, this work is largely concerned with the story of the shrine which attracted so much medieval renown and has recently inspired modern devotion. It has not always been easy to separate the history of the shrine from that of the priory, nor have I always judged it profitable so to do, even at the cost of some slight inconsistency. Further research, notably among the public records and English medieval wills, may well reveal useful points which I have missed, but I trust that the following essay will provide a useful outline of a topic worthy of a good deal more attention than that which ecclesiastical historians have conceded it in the last hundred years. At a later date I hope to study medieval pilgrimages in England more comprehensively and have reserved until then comment on the more general aspects of the cult of Our Lady of Walsingham. I should be most grateful for corrections or additions to this essay and for news of the present whereabouts of Walsingham pilgrim tokens or charters.

My principal thanks are due to Mr and Mrs John Gurney of the Abbey House for their kindness in according me frequent and fullest access to the remains of the priory, and answering various queries regarding it. I am also much indebted to Professor D. Knowles and Professor F. Wormald for reading the draft of this work and making various suggestions for its amelioration, to

PREFACE

Dr R. C. Smail for drawing my attention to the publications of the Palestine Pilgrims' Text Society and to Mr G. R. C. Davies of the British Museum for help in deciphering some obscure passages in the cartulary of Walsingham. For topographical aid I am grateful to Mr R. Rainbird Clarke, Curator of the Norwich Museums, Rev. J. F. Williams archivist to the Lord Bishop of Norwich and Mr A. Bond of Walsingham. Mr Geoffrey Webb, Mr E. A. R. Rahbula, Mr P. Eden and Mr John H. Harvey have kindly solved various architectural queries and Mr S. D. T. Spittle most kindly made the plan of the priory reproduced below. For the plates here reproduced I am indebted to the Cambridge University Press, the British Museum, the Public Record Office, the London Guildhall Museum, the Ashmolean Museum, Oxford, Mr H. L. Bradfer-Lawrence and Mr C. Fisher. For help in collecting photographs of Walsingham pilgrim tokens I must thank Mr P. Lasko, Mr R. Merrifield, Mr H. E. Bocking, Mr C. Fisher and Mr Norman Smedley. Finally I must record my indebtedness to the officials of the Cambridge University Press.

J. C. D.

CAMBRIDGE
June 1955

LIST OF ABBREVIATIONS

Arch. Journ.   *Archaeological Journal*

B.M.   British Museum

Cartul.   Cartulary of Walsingham Priory (British Museum, MS. Cotton, Nero E VII)

C.C.R.   *Calendar of Close Rolls*

C.Ch.R.   *Calendar of Charter Rolls*

C.P.R.   *Calendar of Patent Rolls*

C.Pap.Reg.   *Calendar of Papal Registers*

L. and P.   *Calendar of Letters and Papers, Foreign and Domestic, Henry VIII*

Mon.   W. Dugdale, *Monasticon Anglicanum*, ed. J. Caley, H. Ellis and B. Bandinel, 6 vols. in 8, 1830 (References are to vol. VI, unless otherwise stated.)

Nichols   *Pilgrimages to St Mary of Walsingham and St Thomas of Canterbury* by D. Erasmus, transl. J. G. Nichols (1875).

Norwich Visitations   *Visitations of the Diocese of Norwich, 1492–1532* ed. A. Jessop (Camden Soc.), 1888.

P.R.O.   Public Record Office

Rec. Com.   Record Commission

R.S.   Rolls Series (Chronicles and Memorials of Great Britain and Ireland)

V.C.H.   *Victoria History of the Counties of England*

PART I

HISTORICAL

CHAPTER I

THE ORIGINS OF THE SHRINE

IT is not easy for the modern reader to appreciate how dark was the glass through which medieval man viewed his history. The information at his disposal was frequently scanty and unreliable, with the inevitable result that the picture he saw as he peered into an obscure past differed notably from that lit up by the light of modern research. One might have expected that historical accuracy could at least have been found at such seats of learning as the universities of Oxford and Cambridge, yet by the end of the Middle Ages both of them had antedated their own foundation by centuries, maintaining a connexion with the mythical Prince Cantaber, the semi-mythical Prince Arthur, and with King Alfred and the Emperor Charlemagne, both of whom had been dead three hundred years before there was the slightest sign of university life in England.[1] Similarly, we find the kings of England had long claimed descent from the mythical King Brutus.[2] From this historical disability ecclesiastical institutions were by no means immune. The abbey of Glastonbury, with a more venerable history than that of any other English monastery, developed a quite baseless tradition linking its early years with St Joseph of Arimathaea himself.[3] In such an atmosphere it was not surprising that the

---

[1] H. Rashdall, *The Universities of Europe in the Middle Ages* (ed. F. M. Powicke and A. B. Emden, 3 vols., 1936), III, 5–6, 276.

[2] T. D. Kendrick, *British Antiquity* (1950), 4–7.

[3] J. Armitage Robinson, *Two Glastonbury Legends* (Cambridge Univ. Press, 1926).

THE ORIGINS OF THE SHRINE

famous house of Our Lady of Walsingham had, by the time of the Reformation, somewhat distorted the story of its own beginnings.

In a Book of Hours now in the University Library, Cambridge, a note claims that the original chapel at Walsingham was founded in 1061,[1] and this is elaborated in a ballad on the house, published by Richard Pynson in or soon after 1496.[2] But this very late evidence is squarely contradicted by earlier and much more reliable material, which shows that the origins of the shrine belong to the early half of the twelfth century. The very fine cartulary of Walsingham Priory now in the British Museum[3] furnishes a list of priors, giving both their names and the length of their periods of office which establishes that the priory at Walsingham began in or about 1153,[4] and this is attested by other evidence. The Pynson ballad tells us that the priory at Walsingham was preceded by a chapel built in honour of Our Lady by one Richelde of Fervaques[5] whose son, Geoffrey, converted the place into a priory. This is confirmed by Geoffrey's foundation charter[6]

---

[1] University Library, Cambridge, MS. Ii. vi. 2, fo. 71ʳ; 'anno domini m⁰ sexagesimo primo capella beate marie de Walsyngham in comitatu Norff. fuit fundata et incepta'. The book belongs to the early fifteenth century but this note is rather later. Cf. J. Leland, *Collectanea* (ed. T. Hearne, 1770) IV, 29: '*Walsingham* Sacellum D. Mariae inchoatum tempore Edwardi Confessoris. Deinde tempore Gulielmi Nothi inducti sunt canonici.' Cf. *ibid.* I, 59, 'Galfridus Faverchesse miles fundator.'

[2] For the text of this see Appendix I (below, 124–30); from verse 14 it appears that the ballad belongs to the late fifteenth century.

[3] Cotton MS. Nero E. VII; two folios of deeds in the same hand are in the Bodleian Library, Oxford, MS. Top. Norfolk b. 1.

[4] *Ibid.* fo. 157ᵛ; see Appendix II (below, 131–4).

[5] The early form of the name 'de Favarches' (*Mon.* 73) is perhaps to be identified with Fervaques (dep. Aisne) in Vermandois, or Fervaques (dep. Calvados, arr. Lisieux); Fervaches (dep. Manches) is also possible.

[6] Cartulary fo. 8ʳ = *Mon.* 73: 'Notum sit vobis me dedisse et concessisse

THE EARLY CHAPEL

and may be taken as certain. His deed cannot be closely dated but is the earliest in the cartulary. A confirmation of it[1] is addressed to William, bishop of Norwich (1146–75) by Roger, earl of Clare (1152–73). As Roger was recognized as earl of Hereford by 1156[2] and is not styled by this title in this charter,[3] it seems likely that the latter was drawn up between 1152 and 1156.

Of Richelde little is known, but we have in the Pipe Roll of 1130–1 an invaluable note which suggests that she was a widow in this year. This tells us that one William de Hocton (probably Houghton) rendered account for ten golden marks for the right to have the wife of Geoffrey Fervaques as his wife, with her land, and to have the wardship of her son until the latter could become a knight, and afterwards the son was to hold the land from William.[4] It is difficult to avoid the conclusion that the Geoffrey here mentioned was the father of the founder of Walsingham Priory and the widow mentioned was Richelde, who built the chapel there. This Geoffrey is mentioned in 1108 along with William de Houghton[5] and he also witnesses the foundation charter of Binham Priory (1101–12).[6] A little later, Binham recovered a moiety of Walsingham

Deo et S. Mariae et Edwino clerico meo, ad ordinem religionis, quem ipse providerit instituendum, capellam quam mater mea fundauit in Walsingham in honore perpetuae Virginis Mariae, una cum possessione ecclesiae Omnium Sanctorum ejusdem villae....'

[1] *Ibid.* no. 3.
[2] *Complete Peerage*, III, 244; cf. *ibid.* VI, 500.   [3] *Mon.* 73, no. 3.
[4] 'Willelmus de Hoctona reddit Compotum de x marcas auri pro uxore Gaufridi de Fauarc. habere in uxorem cum terra sua, et filium suum habere in custodia donec possit esse miles et postea idem filius tenere terram de eodem Willelmo', *Pipe Roll 31 Henry I* (Pipe Roll Soc. 1929), p. 94. The largeness of the sum that William was prepared to pay together with Geoffrey's possession of the patronage of the parish church (mentioned in his charter) suggests that the latter was the main landowner of the parish.
[5] *Mon.* III, 348.   [6] B.M., Cott. MS. Claud. D. XIII, fo. 2^r.

THE ORIGINS OF THE SHRINE

against Geoffrey and his priest Warin,[1] and Geoffrey witnessed a gift to Castle Acre before 1130.[2] But the Pipe Roll shows conclusively that he was dead by 1131, so it is quite clear that it was a namesake of his who founded the priory at Walsingham in or about 1153.

This namesake is almost certainly the son of Geoffrey mentioned in the Pipe Roll of 1130–1 as being then under age. This entry implies that Geoffrey II could not have been born before about 1110 at the very earliest, a fact which tells very strongly against 1061 as the date of the foundation of the chapel at Walsingham by Richelde. For if we were to accept this latter date as accurate, we are bound to believe that Richelde was born some twenty years before 1061 (as a child could not found a chapel) and she would therefore be some seventy or eighty years of age when her son Geoffrey was born. It is worth noting that there is no authority for this date of 1061 earlier than the late fifteenth century, and that by this time it was by no means uncommon for some considerable misunderstanding to exist as to the circumstances under which, several centuries earlier, a monastery came into being. The unreliability of Leland on the foundation of Walsingham is shown by his remark that canons were introduced there under William the Conqueror, a statement that is, almost certainly, quite false. Finally, it is to be noted that there is no evidence of Richelde or any of the Fervaques owning land in Walsingham in the period covered by Domesday Book (1066–86).[3]

If we are to accept the evidence of the Pynson ballad that the chapel at Walsingham was founded by Richelde

---

[1] B.M., Cott. MS. Claud. D. xiii, fo. 41ʳ. [2] *Mon.* v, 50.
[3] Domesday Book, fos. 233, 254.

when she was a widow, we must date the event late in her life, unless we presume an earlier marriage than the one to Geoffrey. As we have not the slightest evidence for this, and since it is all but certain that she was a widow in 1130–1, it seems natural to conclude that the first chapel at Walsingham was founded somewhere about this latter date. It should be noted that, if the chapel had existed for any long period as a place of pilgrimage, before it was given over to regular canons, it would almost inevitably have acquired considerable property which one would expect to find mentioned in the cartulary; of this there is little trace.

It is not impossible that the foundation of the priory at Walsingham took place only a very short time after that of the chapel. For Richelde's erection of the Holy House may have been inspired by her son's visit to the Holy Land (which is mentioned in his foundation charter). When this journey took place is not known, but as Geoffrey was under age in 1131 it may well have been as late as the forties of the century, possibly at the time of the Second Crusade (1147–8). In the present state of the evidence all that can safely be said is that the priory of Walsingham was certainly founded by Geoffrey de Fervaques II in or very near 1153 and that the date of the foundation of the chapel by his mother probably lay in the preceding quarter of a century.[1]

A connexion with Geoffrey's visit to the Holy Land is perhaps borne out by the almost certain fact that Richelde's chapel was no ordinary one, but was planned as a reproduction of the House of Nazareth where Our

---

[1] A popular guide-book has connected with Walsingham, 'Balduinus filius Gaufridi et Ricolda mater eius' mentioned in a Bury St Edmunds charter of 1151–4 (*Feudal Documents from the Abbey of Bury St Edmunds*, ed. D. C. Douglas, 1932, no. 78, p. 91); but there seem no grounds for so doing.

THE ORIGINS OF THE SHRINE

Lady had been greeted with the news of her part in the Incarnation by the Archangel Gabriel. This origin of the chapel is very clearly stated in the Pynson ballad[1] which may well be accurate enough here, if not on other details. Such a view receives very strong support from the remarkable fact that this early chapel at Walsingham was regarded with such tremendous veneration that it was preserved intact till the Reformation.[2] In general, medieval folk had very little respect for the buildings of their forefathers, rebuilding them on a larger and, as it seemed to them, a better scale whenever financial resources permitted. As we shall see, so wealthy a priory as Walsingham could very easily have afforded to rebuild Our Lady's chapel in a most sumptuous way and the fact that it was retained and surrounded by a larger building of considerable splendour is a sure sign that it was regarded as a place of exceptional significance.[3] A deliberate imitation of the original Holy House, as we shall see, would provide a very comprehensible explanation of this, and, indeed, is almost the only one which can safely be invoked to explain the facts as we have them. Some little support is given to the theory advanced above by signs of the early importance attached to a statue of St Gabriel. The earliest detailed reference to the places of pilgrimage at Walsingham encountered by the writer—in the Household Accounts for 18 Edward I—makes mention of the statue of St Gabriel[4] which was then apparently in the little chapel. Such an image would have been an almost inevitable accompaniment of a

[1] Below, 125–6. The twelfth-century guides to the Holy Land make it clear that no building claimed to be the original one at this time, though what was thought to have been the site of the latter was venerated.
[2] Below, 102–4.   [3] Ibid.
[4] Below, 39.

THE STATUE OF OUR LADY

replica of the House of Nazareth. If it was later moved elsewhere, this would be natural enough once the statue of Our Lady of Walsingham had reached such eminence as completely to eclipse in interest the chapel itself, which certainly seems to have quickly come to be regarded as largely a setting for the statue.

The statue which made Walsingham famous was one of Our Lady and the Holy Child. It was burnt at the time of the Reformation[1] but what is almost certainly a representation of it is preserved on a seal of the priory[2] and on certain pilgrim badges.[3] There can be no doubt that the statue was of mid- or late twelfth-century date and it is a curious fact, hitherto unnoted, that it bears a close resemblance to that of Our Lady of Rocamadour.[4] It is not certain that this statue was in the original chapel before the foundation of the priory. Not only may it be rather later in date than the chapel, but it does not seem probable that a chapel commemorating the Annunciation would be provided with a statue of Our Lady showing her seated on a throne with the infant Christ on her arm.

However this may be, there can be no doubt that the shrine of Walsingham began as nothing more than a place of private devotion erected by the great lady of the parish probably in the second quarter of the twelfth century. It was not intended as a centre of public worship, the parishioners' spiritual needs being very adequately met at this time by the three churches, All Saints', Little Walsingham, and St Peter's and All Saints', of Great Walsingham. Equally certain is it that, in or about 1153, a small priory of Austin canons was

---

[1] Below, 65.
[2] On the seals of the house see below, 108 ff.
[3] Below, 113-4. [4] Below, 112.

THE ORIGINS OF THE SHRINE

established at Walsingham and given charge of the chapel.[1] It is curious that, whereas Geoffrey de Fervaques's foundation charter envisages the regular life being initiated by 'my clerk Edwy',[2] the confirmation by Earl Roger (which is presumably only a little later in date) speaks of 'my clerks of Walsingham, Ralph and Geoffrey' instituting the new order there. It is possible that Edwy had died in the meantime. The Ralph here mentioned is evidently the one of that name who occurs as the first prior of Walsingham.[3]

There are two possible explanations of this alteration in status of the chapel at Walsingham. It may have been principally due to the very profound veneration for the monastic life prevalent at this time. The reign which saw the foundation of the priory of Walsingham saw, in less than twenty years, the establishment of more religious houses than had been founded in the previous century, and the number of monasteries in England increased fourfold between 1100 and 1216. To sensitive minds the cloister offered a power and joy hardly to be found in the world outside, whilst the intercession of religious was highly prized by the great section of society which continued to live in the world. It was evidently this veneration for monasticism that had led to the foundation of the neighbouring priories of West Acre and Coxford,[4] and it probably inspired the introduction of the monastic life at Walsingham.

On the other hand, another explanation is just possible. Once a local church had become a place of pilgrimage, there were obvious advantages in transferring to the hands of religious who could satisfy the complex demands of such a centre and provide the

---

[1] Above, 4–5.   [2] *Mon.* 73.   [3] Below, 133.
[4] J. C. Dickinson, *The Origin of the Austin Canons* (1950), 149.

THE FOUNDATION OF THE PRIORY

edifying example so specially appropriate there. Thus early in the century the priest in charge of the historic church of Hexham gave it to Austin canons, and other brethren of the order guarded the relics of St Wulfad at Stone and St Eadburgh at Bicester,[1] just as their continental brethren are found at this time in charge of the churches of Sainte-Geneviève of Paris, San Frediano of Lucca and Santiago of Compostella. If the chapel of Walsingham rapidly became at least a local place of pilgrimage, it would have been very natural to entrust it to the care of a community of Austin canons. Whether we take this view or not depends principally on the difficult question of the date at which Walsingham became a centre of public devotion. As we shall see, however, it is to be admitted that there is no clear sign of pilgrimages to the shrine for some decades after the foundation of the priory.

To those acquainted with the nature of medieval historical evidence it will come as no surprise that the story of Walsingham as a pilgrimage centre cannot be written in anything more than outline, partly because the necessary evidence on the question has been destroyed, but more especially because much of it never existed in permanent form. If the library and archives of the priory had survived the Reformation, if we were still able to consult such works as the 'Annals of the chapel of Walsingham', seen by the fifteenth-century chronicler John Capgrave[2] we should be in a much happier condition. As it is, we are driven to rely on the extensive but not very helpful material contained in the cartulary, eked out by isolated references in a variety of other sources of varying degrees of reliability.

[1] *Ibid.* 148–9.   [2] Below, 38–9.

THE ORIGINS OF THE SHRINE

There are three factors which may lie behind the rise to fame of Our Lady's Chapel at Walsingham. First, of course, is the attraction which the shrine may have exerted as a copy of the Holy House about the time the mellifluous voice of Saint Bernard was stirring up popular devotion to the Holy Land by his preaching for the Second Crusade. It is not difficult to sense the effect on medieval Norfolk of the establishment, within its bounds, of so clear-cut a connexion with the Holy Land in general, and in particular with the Blessed Virgin whose praises were so often on St Bernard's lips and whose name was borne by all the great Cistercian abbeys now springing up in such numbers all over the Latin world.

To this it is just possible that we ought to add the attraction of the wells which adjoined the original chapel of Our Lady of Walsingham. As is almost inevitable, medieval historical evidence being what it is, their history is very ill documented, and it is not certain whether the absence of early evidence of their popularity means that this never existed or merely that proof of it has not survived. The first reference to them found by the writer occurs in a list of canons of the house given in the cartulary[1] where we are told that Thomas Gatele, a fifteenth-century subprior of Walsingham, as a boy fell into 'the well of Blessed Mary' and, after being taken out as dead, was restored to life by a miracle or Our Lady.[2] It is a matter of opinion whether this is to be interpreted as implying general public access to the well or as merely one more example of the perennial tendency of small boys to turn up in unexpected places. The well is, presumably, one of the 'tweyne wells' mentioned in the Pynson ballad, still to be seen some

[1] Below, Appendix III (135–40). [2] Below, 136.

hundred and sixty feet east of the church. The ballad makes it quite clear that healing was one of the phenomena associated with the shrine,[1] but does not, like Erasmus,[2] specifically connect this with the wells. Evidence being so thin, it would clearly be unwise to base any important conclusion on it, and it is likely enough that it was the statue of Our Lady that was the original attraction.[3] It is at least curious that the site at Nazareth by which the house at Walsingham is believed to have been inspired was also connected with a well. The medieval pilgrims' reports mostly mention it. The account of the Russian abbot, Daniel,[4] tells us that 'the holy Virgin received the first announcement from the Archangel at the well of the first Annunciation...a good bowshot from the town'; the well is described as 'very deep...with very cold water' and had, at that time, built over it a round church dedicated to the Archangel Gabriel. Mention of this well probably derives ultimately from the apocryphal Book of James.[5]

Almost certainly much the most important factor in the rise of Walsingham to popularity was the growing devotion to the statue of Our Lady there. Almost every church at this time had such a statue, and this work is not concerned with the difficult problem of why some of them became so much more venerated than others.

[1] Below, 128. [2] Below, 92.
[3] See below, 14–18. A well, whose supply may be connected with that of the wells in the priory grounds, was found when remains of a building overlapping the site of the present Anglican shrine were partially excavated. It is quite likely that it is the 'well called Cabbokeswell' mentioned in a deed of 1387. (Cartulary fo. 27, imperfectly printed in *Arch. Journ.* XIII (1856), 131.) From the medieval notes on this deed which follow, it seems very likely that at some period the priory had constructed an almonry near the well which may have been the building whose foundations were discovered when the modern shrine was built.
[4] *Palestine Pilgrims' Text Soc.* IV (2), 71.
[5] *The Apocryphal New Testament*, trs. M. R. James (1924), 43.

THE ORIGINS OF THE SHRINE

Of this as a fact there can be no doubt. Sometimes such popularity was of unexpectedly rapid growth, as when, in 1310, at Bridlington Priory's chapel at Fraisthorpe by reason of devotion to 'a certain new image of the Virgin' there 'suddenly and unexpectedly' arose new offerings on what was evidently a fairly considerable scale.[1] But in general, achievement of popularity seems to have been a gradual process. It is certain that the statue of Our Lady at Walsingham was incomparably the most important shrine of its kind in medieval England, but it is difficult to get any very clear idea as to how it attained this ascendancy.

So ordinary an event as a pilgrimage to a shrine attracted no considerable attention in chronicles or records, in just the same way as the audience at a cricket match or concert today leaves little written trace of itself to delight the future social historian. When such unpublished sources as the Household and Wardrobe Accounts have been fully ransacked, it will be possible to add some few details of the later pilgrimages to Walsingham so far as the royal household was concerned, but folk of lesser degree have left only the scantiest traces of the thousands of visits they undoubtedly made to the shrine of Our Lady there. For knowledge of the important first hundred years of the priory's history we are largely dependent on evidence from the cartulary. Valuable as are its early deeds, they throw very little light on many aspects of the house's life, and the fact that they have not yet found an editor further diminishes their present value.

One point, however, is perfectly clear—the very small financial importance of Walsingham up to the

[1] *Chartulary of Bridlington Priory*, ed. W. T. Lancaster (Leeds, 1912), 448-9.

THE POVERTY OF THE EARLY PRIORY

middle of the thirteenth century. Had it been a major pilgrimage centre from its early days, the house would certainly have acquired considerable property by this time, but the evidence shows quite clearly that it had not succeeded in doing this. According to a late note in the cartulary, Geoffrey of Fervaques 'fowndyth the chyrche off the seyd priory and he gaffe it to the chapel off owr Lady with al the grownd with inne the seyte off the seyd place, wyth the chyrch off the seyde ton qwych than was taxid c*s*. be yer. And with viii acr. dim. off land with xx*s*. of yerly rent to be payd owte of hys maner in the seyd Walsyngham. The yeri [*sic*] valwe of alle this seyd fundacion, except the offeryng of the seyd chapel of our lady, passyd not x marcs.'[1] This tradition of the lack of estates in the priory's early years is fully supported by the detailed specification of the house's possessions drawn up by Prior William in 1250.[2] Apart from the priory and its precinct the main possessions there enumerated were the church of All Saints, Little Walsingham, 20*s*. yearly from a mill in the village, 8½ acres in Snoring with its pasture, the church of All Saints, Great Walsingham,[3] and 40*d*. of land in Walsingham given by William, brother of King Henry (d. 1164), to which are added a dozen gifts of land (the largest of which was only six acres) and one or two small rents.

The only effective clue, located by the writer, to the relative income of the house at this time is provided by the assessment for the feudal aid of 1235–6,[4] which gives the same impression of mediocrity. Of the local houses

---

[1] *Mon.* 70 = Cartul. fo. 5ᵛ.
[2] Bod. Lib. Oxf., Norfolk Charters, 554.
[3] The original deed of gift of this by Rowland 'de Terra Vasta' is now B.M., Charters, Topham 42. Very few deeds of the priory are known to have survived.
[4] *Book of Fees*, 566. Bromholm was assessed at £5.

of Austin canons, Butley easily headed the list with £13. 6s. 8d., followed by Coxford and West Acre assessed at £5, whilst Walsingham, with St Peter's (Ipswich), Pentney and Blythburgh, was rated at £3. 6s. 8d., Bricett at £2 and Wormgay at £1. 6s. 8d. This is in striking contrast to the situation shown in the Valor Ecclesiasticus of 1535 where Walsingham figures as easily the richest house of the order in Norfolk. It is, of course, true that we cannot dismiss the possibility that there were quite considerable gifts in these early years which were spent in ways that have left no trace in our records. Thus casual offerings at this period may well have been devoted to increasing the number of brethren in the house or to building operations on a considerable scale. Unhappily we have no clear evidence on this sort of expenditure, though building operations were certainly in progress in the late twelfth century, and the cartulary shows the convent enlarging its precinct in the time of Gilbert de Clare, earl of Gloucester and Hereford (1230–62) and his son William.[1] But this is not necessarily of any great significance and, as we shall see, at the end of the century, though Walsingham has certainly improved its position, it is far from being a place of great wealth.

Equally fragile is the evidence of the hospital of Beck which was founded in 1224, it is said for the reception of pilgrims visiting Walsingham,[2] though no evidence has been produced to show that this was its original purpose. The only people whose movements at this time can be regularly ascertained are the kings of England,

[1] Cartul., fos. 12ᵛ–14ᵛ. Hubert de Burgh gave the church of Oulton 'pro anima Aleysie matris nostre in ecclesia de Walsingham quiescentis', ibid. fo. 91ʳ.

[2] V.C.H., Norfolk, II, 438; the statement may be based on a misreading of T. Tanner, Notitia Monastica (ed. J. Nasmith, 1787), Norfolk, IV.

HENRY III AND WALSINGHAM

who, in the matter of pilgrimage, may or may not have resembled their subjects. The rather sketchy itinerary of Henry II (d. 1189) shows no trace of his having visited Walsingham,[1] and it is certain that Richard I (d. 1199)[2] and John (d. 1216)[3] were never there. It can, of course, be argued that such negative evidence amounts to little, that Henry and Richard were busy kings who spent much of their time abroad and John was little given to visiting shrines. To which it may be replied that, as Henry III and Edward I were to show, in this as in other matters, where there was the will there was the way.

There seems little doubt that Walsingham's rise to national fame was due more to Henry III than to anyone else. Whatever the king's faults, distaste for devotional exercises was not among them, and it was not surprising that he took an early opportunity to venerate the relic of the Holy Cross owned by Bromholm Priory which lay some twenty-six miles east of Walsingham. The relic had been acquired about 1220 and within the next few years the fame it attracted was sufficient to be a subject of comment in one or two of the leading chronicles of the age.[4] Henry is first found at Bromholm on 5 and 6 April 1226 and on the latter day he granted the priory a fair, to be held on the vigil, day and morrow of the feast of the Holy Cross.[5] The two previous days the King had spent at Walsingham[6] and on 4 April he had granted the priory the right to hold a weekly market at Walsingham[7] and also a fair on the

[1] R. W. Eyton, *Court, Household and Itinerary of Henry II* (1878), *passim*.
[2] *Itinerary of Richard I*, Pipe Roll Soc. (n.s.), XIII (1935).
[3] *Rotuli Litterarum Patentium* (Rec. Com.), Introduction.
[4] F. Wormald, 'The Rood of Bromholm', *Journ. Warburg Inst.* I, 31–45.
[5] *Rotuli Litterarum Clausarum*, II, 105.
[6] *Ibid.*   [7] *Ibid.*

THE ORIGINS OF THE SHRINE

vigil and day of the Holy Cross.[1] These grants suggest that Walsingham was of only secondary importance to Bromholm. Walsingham's fair was only for two days and was to be held on the same day as that of Bromholm, not on a feast of Our Lady as was later the case and as might have been expected had the shrine already been important. Yet this visit was but the first of many paid by a king, and was made by one who seems to have fallen in love with the place.

We find Henry next at Walsingham on 5 August 1229[2] and again on 3 July 1232 when he gave the prior forty oak trees for the work of the Church,[3] and letters of protection.[4] Two years later Henry gave the priory twenty oak trees 'to make a certain building' (*camera*)[5] and in 1235 he was at Walsingham again.[6] On 6 June 1238 he came yet once more,[7] having spent the previous night at Bromholm, and in 1242 was at Walsingham from 24 to 26 March after a visit to Bromholm two days earlier.[8] Henry gave the canons a yearly grant of 40*s*. mentioned in 1229,[9] and various gifts of wax and tapers in 1239, 1240, 1241, 1242 and 1244.[10] Several of the latter were considerable; that of 1241 gave no less than 3000 tapers to be offered in the chapel of St Mary at Walsingham on the feast of the Assumption. In 1242 the Pipe Rolls show that he had given substantial gifts of wax to Bury St Edmunds, Norwich and Bromholm, but the largest share went to Walsingham—100 pounds of wax and 500 tapers valued at 118*s*. 8*d*.[11] In March 1245 the

---

[1] *Rotuli Litterarum Clausarum*, II, 105.   [2] *C.C.R.* (*1227–31*), 199.
[3] *Ibid.* (*1231–4*), 82.   [4] *C.P.R.* (*1225–32*), 488.
[5] *C.C.R.* (*1231–4*), 379.   [6] *Ibid.* (*1234–7*), 59.
[7] *Ibid.* (*1237–42*), 58.   [8] *Ibid.* 407, 345.
[9] *Cal. Liberate Rolls* (*1226–40*), 118, 149.
[10] *Ibid.* (*1226–40*), 398; (*1240–45*), 9, 66, 114, 143, 245.
[11] *The Pipe Roll of 26 Henry III* (*1241–2*), ed. H. L. Cannon, 190.

king was at Bromholm and Walsingham yet again[1] as he was in 1248.[2] In 1246 had come the interesting and generous gift of 20 marks to make a golden crown and place it on the image of St Mary of Walsingham.[3] On 13 March 1251 the king ordered a certain embroidered chasuble to be sent quickly to him at Walsingham[4] and he is found there on the 25th (Lady Day) when he granted the priory a great fair to be held on the vigil and day of the feast of the Nativity of St Mary and six days after, a substantial favour in return for which the convent was to have a wax candle weighing two pounds, continually burning before the great altar of their church.[5] March 17, 1256, saw Henry at Walsingham[6] and three days later he was at Bromholm.[7] On 16 March 1255, when at Thetford, he had issued a charter confirming a number of smallish benefactions to the priory[8]. After this remarkable series of visits it is a little surprising that the king is only found once more at Walsingham—in September 1272 when he may have stayed several days, as letters from there dated the 22nd and 29th of the month have survived.[9] In some ways Henry's most valuable benefaction to Walsingham was the deep devotion to the shrine implanted in his son Edward I (1272–1307).

[1] *C.P.R.* (*1242–7*), 295. [2] *Ibid.* (*1247–58*), 10.
[3] *Cal. Liberate Rolls* (*1245–51*), 18.
[4] *C.C.R.* (*1247–51*), 423. Cf. *Cal. Liberate Rolls* (*1245–51*), 354; it had cost £13. 15s. 2d.
[5] *C.Ch.R.*, (*1226–57*), 354; he was there on Mar. 28, *C.P.R.* (*1247–58*), 91.
[6] *C.C.R.* (*1254–6*), 286.
[7] *C.P.R.* (*1247–58*), 466.
[8] *Mon.* 73, no. 6. The acquisitions are minor and miscellaneous including small rents, a few villeins, three-quarters of the advowson of St Andrew's, Burnham and some gifts of land of which the chief were of twenty-five and sixty acres.
[9] *C.P.R.* (*1266–72*), 679; *C.C.R.* (*1268–72*), 527; *C.Ch.R.* II, 184.

THE ORIGINS OF THE SHRINE

Edward's attachment to Walsingham was of long standing. We are told by a reliable chronicler that, on one occasion during his youth, Edward was playing chess in a vaulted room when he suddenly moved away and immediately a large stone from the roof fell on the spot where he had been sitting 'because of which miracle he ever afterwards most ardently honoured our Lady of Walsingham', a decision which clearly implies previous knowledge of her cult.[1] Gough's magnificent *Itinerary*[2] shows evident signs of the reality of the devotion to Walsingham, in later days, of a king who only twice visited Bromholm.[3] Edward is found at Walsingham on no less than twelve occasions. He was there first as a king on Palm Sunday 1277 and again between 5 and 8 January 1281, thus including the feast of the Epiphany. On this occasion Edward confirmed the priory's possessions, its ecclesiastical property being specified in detail.[4] In 1289 the king and his queen, having returned to England from Gascony, went to pay a vow first at Bury St Edmunds and then at Walsingham,[5] where they are found on 24 September. It is tempting to speculate whether the king may not now have made a special vow to visit the shrine of Our Lady here, for from now on his visits are so frequent as to be almost annual.[6]

---

[1] 'Cum adhuc adolescens esset et cum quodam milite in camera testudinata ludo scaccarii occuparetur, subito, nulla occasione praestita, inter ludendum surgens discessit, et ecce! lapis immensae magnitudinis qui sedentem conquassasset, cecidit in eundum locum quo sederat; propter quod miraculum, Beatam Mariam apud Walsyngham semper postea propensius honorabat. Ei revera attribuebat quod periculum istud evasit.' William Rishanger, *Chronica* (R.S. 79), II, 76–7 = Thomas of Walsingham, *Historia Anglorum* (R.S. 79), I, 9.

[2] H. Gough, *Itinerary of King Edward the First* (2 vols., Paisley, 1900), *passim*.

[3] In 1277 and 1285 (*op. cit.*).   [4] *Mon.* 74.

[5] John of Oxenedes, *Chron.* (R.S. 13), 273.

[6] See Gough, *op. cit., passim*.

EDWARD I AND THE SHRINE

His chancery is found at Walsingham on 10–11 May 1292, from 26 February to 4 March 1294 (when he granted a licence to alienate in mortmain),[1] and from 28 to 30 January 1296 when the king is known to have been on pilgrimage.[2] A few days later, on the Feast of the Purification (2 February) representatives of the king and of the count of Flanders swore acceptance of a treaty in the chapel of Our Lady at Walsingham.[3] This feast seems to have been the principal feast of Our Lady at Walsingham, and Edward assisted at its observance the next year (1297). Further visits followed on 13 May 1298, 20 January 1299, 14–15 May 1300 (when we have records of the king's offerings, of one made on behalf of the queen,[4] and ten days later those by the young prince, Edward).[5] The king came again on 30 March 1302, and for the last time on 1 February 1305, staying on this occasion till the 3rd, thus again being present for the feast of the Purification.

The very restricted nature of thirteenth-century evidence sheds next to no light on visits of the less illustrious to Walsingham, and, though unexplored records may add a little to our knowledge, it is unlikely that we shall ever obtain more than occasional very fleeting glimpses of such pilgrims to the shrine at this time. Medieval records are largely concerned with privileges, property, disorders and royal finance. The first two are irrelevant to our purpose, and the last two concern it little. It is significant of the perversity of our sources, that mention of the first member of the general public known to have visited the shrine has survived purely because he

---

[1] *C.P.R.* (*1292–1301*), 83. It concerns land in Burnham and Salle.
[2] Barthol. Cotton, *Hist. Angl.* (R.S. 16), 316–17.
[3] *Annales monastici* (R.S. 36) IV, 529.
[4] Below, 39.   [5] *Ibid.*

THE ORIGINS OF THE SHRINE

became involved in legal proceedings. In 1261 John le Chaumpeneys and his mother were going on pilgrimage to Walsingham when John was attacked by his landlord at Bintree and in defence accidentally killed him.[1] Had he not done so, he would have disappeared as completely from history's page as the hundreds of his social contemporaries who made peaceful journeys to the shrine. So far as details of offerings are concerned, we have only the bare entries in a handful of medieval private accounts mostly of the aristocracy and mostly compiled in the last two centuries of Walsingham's history. Thus for most of its history and particularly in its early stages the rise of the flood of pilgrims to Walsingham and the nature and extent of their benefactions can only be traced in the very barest of outlines.

An invaluable indication of the financial state of things is found in the particulars furnished by the Taxatio of Pope Nicholas (1291). It is clear from this that, although Walsingham was, even then, far from being a wealthy house, its position since the assessment of 1235–6 had improved. Its temporalities—almost all in Norfolk—were assessed at £78. 17s. 0¾d. being slightly more than those of Bromholm (£74. 17s. 7d.); whilst the 'offerings in the chapel of Our Lady' were rated at £20.[2] Walsingham was now among the middle-sized houses of Austin canons, even if very far away from the enormously wealthy position it occupied at the time of its suppression, when it was the second richest monastery in Norfolk, surpassed only by the cathedral priory of Norwich.[3]

[1] *C.P.R. (1258–68)*, 182.
[2] *Taxatio Ecclesiastica* (Rec. Com.), 108–9, 94–5, 93. I have not noted any estimate of offerings at Bromholm at this time, though at the Dissolution they had sunk to the very low figure of £5. 12s. 9d.
[3] A. Savine, *English Monasteries on the Eve of the Dissolution* (1909), 278–9.

GROWTH OF THE PRIORY

A possible further indication of the improved position of the house is provided by the architectural evidence, which suggests that in the latter half of the thirteenth century the refectory and cloister were probably rebuilt and a western tower added to the church about the end of the period.[1] It was perhaps this architectural activity which led to the house being heavily in debt when Archbishop Pecham visited it in 1280.[2]

[1] Below, 74 ff.
[2] Cartul. fo. 12ʳ. He allowed the priory to serve the Church of All Saints, Little Walsingham, by a suitable chaplain, 'donec sitis a debitorum sarcina liberati, in quibus nuper domum vestram visitantes nos invenimus multipliciter gravatos et oppressos'.

CHAPTER II

THE PROGRESS OF PILGRIMAGE

ALTHOUGH the readily available evidence for this period continues to be scrappy in the extreme, it suffices to show that, from the late fourteenth century on, the shrine of Our Lady of Walsingham was of national importance. At first, signs of royal patronage are disappointingly small. Edward II seems to have first visited Walsingham as king 6–8 October 1315,[1] though six and a half years earlier, at the instance of Queen Isabella, he had granted the house the valuable licence to acquire in mortmain lands and rents to the yearly value of £40,[2] probably a symptom both of royal favour and of the rising resources of the priory. In 1326 letters of 2–6 February show that the king was at Walsingham for the feast of the Purification.[3] Edward III was a frequent visitor in the early years of his reign, the royal chancery being at Walsingham 19–20 September[4] and 9 November[5] 1328, 26–28 June[6] and 21 August[7] 1331, 20–30 August 1333,[8] 6–8 October 1334,[9] 13 March 1339,[10] 12–20 February 1336.[11] Late in 1343 the king returned to England from France and went on pilgrimage, first to Canterbury on foot, and then riding to

[1] *C.C.R.* (*1313–8*), 249–53. For his offerings at this time see below, 40.
[2] *C.P.R.* (*1307–13*), 156.
[3] *C.C.R.* (*1323–7*), 444, 448, 544, 545.
[4] *C.P.R.* (*1327–30*), 319, 321; see below, 40.
[5] *C.P.R.* (*1327–30*), 421.
[6] *C.P.R.* (*1330–4*), 148, 150; *C.C.R.* (*1330–3*), 247.
[7] *C.P.R.* (*1330–4*), 466.   [8] *C.C.R.* (*1330–3*), 75, 131.
[9] *Ibid.* 265, 343.   [10] *C.P.R.* (*1334–8*), 93.
[11] *Ibid.* 222–6, 281; *C.C.R.* (*1333–7*), 541–3, 645–7.

FOURTEENTH-CENTURY PILGRIMS

Gloucester and Walsingham.[1] Rather surprisingly the Chancery Enrolments show no sign of Edward's having visited Walsingham in the remaining thirty-four years of his reign. After this time easily accessible evidence on royal movements is for a century and a half exceptionally meagre. Richard II and his queen were on pilgrimage in the May and June of 1383, visiting Walsingham and Bury St Edmunds.[2]

Meanwhile some eminent foreign visitors came. In 1332 we have mention of 'the old Queen' coming from Walsingham.[3] In March 1361, John, duke of Brittany, received £9 from the king for expenses incurred by a pilgrimage to Walsingham,[4] and in the following May licence was granted to the duke of Anjou to visit the shrines of St Thomas of Canterbury and Our Lady of Walsingham.[5] In April 1363 Gerard le Boucher, described as 'Burgess of Compiègne, hostage', was licenced to visit Our Lady of Walsingham and St John of Beverley, as was Amanda de Landa, burgess of Douai;[6] in May, Guy, count of St Pol, had similar permission to go to Walsingham.[7] The following year David Bruce was given safe conduct by the king to make the same pilgrimage.[8] In 1383 John of Gaunt gave safe conduct to Sir James Lindsay, a Scottish knight, and to a hundred people riding in his company, for various pilgrimages including Canterbury and Walsingham.[9] In 1380 and 1382 he had given permission to Sir Bernard Brocas to

[1] Adam of Murimuth, *Chron. Contin.* (R.S. 93), 135.
[2] *Polychronicon Ranulfi Higden* (R.S. 41) IX, 20.
[3] Hist. MSS. Com., 11th Rep. III, 213.
[4] T. Rymer, *Foedera*, III (2), 605 = Syllabus (ed. T. D. Hardy), I, 416.
[5] *Syllabus* (ed. T. D. Hardy), I, 417.
[6] *Ibid.* 427. [7] *Ibid.* 428.
[8] *Ibid.* 431.
[9] *John of Gaunt's Register 1379–83* (Camden Soc., 1937), ed. E. C. Lodge and R. Somerville, no. 1194.

'hunt reasonably' on his way to and from Walsingham.[1] A glimpse of the wealth of the shrine a little earlier is afforded by the curious and elaborate petition of the canons of Walsingham against the proposal to establish a house of Franciscans in the town (*c.* 1346).[2] Amongst other things this tells us that to safeguard the jewels offered in honour of Our Lady and their other possessions from thieves, the canons found it necessary to close the priory gate at night. About the same time the Slipper Chapel at Houghton was built and may be a further sign of the established popularity of the shrine by this date.[3]

This evidence is reinforced from other sources. Written signs of the hundreds of pilgrims of low degree who flocked to Walsingham at this time are still of the scantiest, though of the fact itself there can be no reasonable doubt, even if we are still straitly limited to occasional glimpses of the part Our Lady of Walsingham played in the life of ordinary people. In or about 1343 some fishermen from Winterton, having lost their nets at sea, implored divine aid that 'by reverence of the image of Blessed Mary at Walsingham and by the merits of St Edmund' they might be recovered.[4] In 1364 the pilgrims to Walsingham included not only David Bruce but one Philip Crikyere who, by rights, should have been in Hertford jail whither he had been consigned after being indicted of extortion. But he was evidently a persuasive character, for he secured his keeper's licence to go on pilgrimage to Walsingham. Unfortunately, on his way back Philip got involved in a

[1] *John of Gaunt's Register 1379–83*, nos. 252, 645.
[2] Cartul. fos. 160r–161r, printed in *Arch. Journ.* XXVI (1869), 169–73; cf. *Norfolk Archaeology*, XXV, 269–71; the friary was founded in 1347–8.
[3] See Appendix IV, below (141–2).
[4] *Memor. of St Edmund's Abbey* (R.S. 96), III, 319.

brawl, in the course of which he killed a man and thus further interested the powers of the law.[1] Of similarly unimportant status were the two jurors who in 1367 are said to have remembered the birth of one Adam de Wolveton, because on the Monday after it they started on their journey to Walsingham on pilgrimage.[2]

By this time the growth of English literature gives a few typically erratic references to the history of the shrine. Archbishop FitzRalph of Armagh in a sermon in 1346 spoke temperately of the dangers attendant on the cult of, *inter alia*, 'our dere lauedy of Walsyngham'.[3] Langland's *Vision of Piers the Plowman* (*c.* 1362) mentions that 'Heremites on an heep with hoked staues, Wenten to Walsyngham',[4] whilst his Avarice swears repentance and vows to 'wenden to Walsyngham and my wyf also, And bidde the Rode of Bromeholme brynge me oute of dette'.[5] Indirect tribute to the importance of Walsingham at this time is furnished by the violent attacks on it made by the Lollards, noted by the chroniclers. Knighton's *Chronicon* under 1382 notes that the Lollards inveighed against what they crudely called 'the wyche of Walsingham'.[6] Thomas of Walsingham tells us that the pilgrimages they singled out for attack were those to Walsingham and to the Cross at the north door of St Paul's Cathedral[7] as does Capgrave[8] (*c.* 1453), whilst Pecock's *Repressor* (*c.* 1449) records their contention, 'it is vein waast and idil forto trotte to Wasingam rather than to ech other place in which an ymage of Marie is'.[9]

---

[1] *C.P.R.* (*1361–4*), 473–4.
[2] *Calendar of Inquisitions post mortem*, XI, no. 231.
[3] G. R. Owst, *Literature and Pulpit in Medieval England* (Cambridge, 1930), 141; cf. 145.
[4] *Piers the Plowman*, ed. W. E. Skeat (1886), Text B, Prologue, 53–4.
[5] *Ibid.* Text B, v, 230–1. [6] *Chronicon* (R.S. 92), II, 183.
[7] *Hist. Anglic.* (R.S. 28), I, 188.
[8] *Liber de illustribus Henricis* (R.S. 7), 252. [9] R.S. 19, I, 194.

At the priory itself, the main signs of its wide repute at this time must have been the extensive rebuilding certainly now begun, involving the erection of a new church of great magnificence, the scheme being in full swing under Prior John Snoring (1374–1401).[1] The aspect of Snoring's priorate, however, which attracted most contemporary notice was his protracted and rather mysterious feud with the bishop of Norwich.

The first sign of trouble in the offing is found in a letter of 6 October 1382,[2] wherein the king ordered the canons of Walsingham not to attempt anything that might prejudice his rights or those of Roger, son and heir of Edmund Mortimer, earl of March,[3] or the laws and customs of the realm or the foundation of the house; it had been reported to the king that the prior 'fearing not the pain of perjury, has without craving or obtaining licence of the king or earl procured letters of the Pope to be made abbot and to rule the same (house)...in the name of abbot...contrary to the founder's will, which would tend not only to the contempt of the king and to the prejudice of the said earl but to overset the rules and constitutions of the priory and to impoverish the same'. The papal bull mentioned has not survived, but we shall see reason to believe that the rather remarkably vigorous opposition which the prior's action so clearly aroused was due to a cause unmentioned in the royal letters. We may here note in passing that the conversion of a priory into an abbey would not necessarily involve the diminution of royal or patronal rights nor involve Walsingham in expenses it could not afford. Nor is it certain that the step would grossly infringe the ordinances of the house or the founder's intention. One or

---

[1] Below, 75–6. [2] *C.C.R.* (*1381–3*), 161.
[3] Patron of the priory at this time.

THE SEARCH FOR ABBATIAL RANK

two cases are known of a founder of a house of Austin canons stipulating that it should not become an abbey, as for example at Cartmel,[1] but it is far from established that any such stipulation was made here.

On 6 March of the next year (1383) the Close Rolls refer again to the matter, one John Yarmouth 'monk of Walsingham abbey' (*sic*) being ordered to give security not to go abroad or attempt there anything that would tend to the prejudice of the king and his people or law or to a breach of the laws of the realm.[2] For nearly a year there was a pause, and one would give much to know the content of the confabulations in the chapterhouse at Walsingham in these months. That trouble was smouldering and was not extinguished is shown by letters patent wherein the king, as guardian of the young Roger de Mortimer, patron of the priory, appointed the subprior of Walsingham as custodian of the priory, 'divers contentions having arisen between the subprior and prior who is desirous to obtain the position of abbot therein and to that end expends its revenues and possessions wastefully'.[3] This was on 1 March 1384 and on the same day the king appointed his chancellor with the keeper of the rolls and three others to inquire concerning 'trespasses and other offences in the priory of St Mary, Walsingham', where divers quarrels had arisen between the brethren to the dissipation of its revenues, the diminution of its worship and the prejudice of Roger de Mortimer.[4]

Prior Snoring seems to have acted quickly and temporarily made his peace with the king; for, eight days later, those appointed to inquire concerning 'trespasses,

---

[1] J. C. Dickinson, *The Origins of the Austin Canons* (1950), 156–7.
[2] *C.C.R.* (*1381–3*), 283–4.   [3] *C.P.R.* (*1381–5*), 383.
[4] *Ibid.* 421.

extortions, maintenance of quarrels, dilapidations, charges to the decrease of divine worship in the priory of St Mary of Walsingham and withdrawal of alms and works of piety appointed of old times' had their commission annulled, since Prior John Snoring had found three sureties of 1000 marks each, that, until the next Parliament, he would keep the priory and possessions without waste or alienation and not go to or send to the Roman court;[1] on the same day letters patent record the the revocation of the grant of custody to the subprior.[2] On 1 April 1384 the bishop of Norwich succeeded in extracting from Prior Snoring a sworn affirmation that he did not intend to use abbatial rights, including the ring and staff, nor to appeal to Rome.[3]

What happened next is not clear. Prior Snoring was clearly a man of determination who may well have felt that he was being persecuted by an unholy combination of bishop and king and have sought redress from the Holy See, but the course of events in the next five years has not been discovered by the writer. However, the removal of Prior Snoring by the bishop of Norwich is mentioned in letters patent of 21 May 1389. These gave the custody of the priory of Walsingham to a body composed of the priors of Coxford and Wymondham, a knight and two clerks. They were to inspect, audit and direct its financial affairs and notify the king if they had any difficulty in reforming abuses; it was noted that the prior had appealed to Rome against sentence of removal.[4] On 25 June fresh custodians were added, it being enjoined that no canon of the house be

---

[1] C.C.R. (1381–5), 433–4.   [2] C.P.R. (1381–5), 389.
[3] The original deed—somewhat damaged—is Bodl. Lib. Oxf., Norfolk Charters, 558.
[4] C.P.R. (1388–92), 36.

appointed to administer it or to rule or dispose of its rents.[1]

On 22 October of the same year, the bishop of Norwich took the disturbing step of appointing John of Hereford, canon of Walsingham, to be prior of the house, on the grounds that collation had devolved to the diocesan by reason of the long absence of the prior.[2] Soon after—on 18 November 1389—Prior Snoring secured royal permission to go to the Roman court to defend his right to the priory.[3] This was no easy matter, and eighteen months later—on 5 June 1391—we find him licensed to prosecute to a conclusion in the Roman court his suit which had long been pending, a knight and two citizens of London having stood surety for a thousand marks each that during his stay he would not attempt anything against the king or the law and customs of the realm.[4]

It seems that Prior Snoring was now defending his right to be prior of Walsingham (as the letters patent of 18 November suggest) and not his original petition for the priory to be converted into an abbey (as is implied in the rather obscure note attached to the list of priors in the cartulary).[5] But, as this note in the cartulary shows, Snoring was ultimately restored to office. However, the end of the contest was not yet. In 1398 we find that John had again appealed to Rome, this time against a decision of the official of the court of Canterbury that he should pay 5 marks to the bishop of Norwich, a sentence he only accepted when threatened with papal excommunication.[6]

---

[1] *Ibid.* 73–4.
[2] Norwich Episcopal Registers, vi, fos. 140ᵛ–141ᵛ.
[3] *C.P.R.* (*1388–92*), 152.   [4] *Ibid.* 424.
[5] Below, 134.
[6] *C. Pap. Reg.* v, 159–60.

The contest ended abruptly in 1400. Archbishop Arundel came to Walsingham on metropolitical visitation, found the prior there 'deeply ensnared in a great variety of defects' and ordered his removal from office. The prior submitted and the archbishop sweetened the pill by granting him a good pension and exemption for life from his old foe, the bishop of Norwich, and from the prior of the house.[1]

The history of the above struggle, when examined closely, shows certain curious features. The hints of the heavy financial expenditure by Prior Snoring are worth noting: his proceedings at Rome may well have been costly, as the cartulary note recorded, but it is very likely that expenses at this time were, in part, due to the heavy building expenditure incurred by Prior Snoring which is known to have taken place at this time,[2] though unmentioned in any of the documents just quoted. From the complaints made against the prior it would seem likely that the not inconsiderable resources of Walsingham were so strained that he employed funds bequeathed for other purposes to close the financial gap; 'the diminution of worship' alleged may well refer to either appropriation of chantry bequests by the prior or possibly a reduction in the size of the convent. There can be no doubt that the prior incurred considerable expenditure, against the will of at least part of the convent. But it is extremely unlikely that more than a part of this was spent in the legal expenses involved in the attempt to convert the priory into an abbey, expensive though the cost of this seems to have been.

For the medieval monastery to get into financial trouble was not uncommon, but this alone seldom disturbed the king and the diocesan in the way that

[1] *Memorials of St Edmund's* (R.S. 96), III, 185. [2] Below, 75–6.

THE SEARCH FOR ABBATIAL RANK

Prior Snoring's activities, whatever they may have been, clearly upset Richard II and Bishop Henry of Norwich. Placing the struggle against the background of the times, it is difficult to avoid the conjecture that the violent opposition of king and bishop to the prior of Walsingham was not caused by any of the actions mentioned in their official deeds, but by an attempt on Snoring's part to obtain for his abbey from the pope the great privilege of exemption from episcopal visitation. Such an action would be violently resented by any normal medieval bishop of Norwich, involving, as it did, the removal from diocesan control of one of the greatest monasteries of his diocese. Whilst the king, as is well known, was so sensitive to anti-papal feeling as to re-enact at this time the Statute of Provisors[1] and the Statute of Praemunire[2] which in theory banned papal provisions and certain important appeals to the papal courts.[3]

From what we have already seen, it is quite clear that by the fifteenth century Walsingham had become a shrine of national importance. It is all the more to be regretted therefore that the available evidence for this period still remains far from adequate. Despite the magnificent windfall of the Paston Letters, comparatively little reference is found to the shrine at this time, the Chancery Enrolments and chronicles of the day proving notoriously inadequate, whilst more hopeful sources remain unedited. For the early part of the century only a few brief glimpses of pilgrims to the shrine have been found.

[1] Passed in 1351, re-enacted in 1390.
[2] Passed in 1353, re-enacted in 1393.
[3] See C. Davies, 'The Statute of Provisors of 1351' in *History* (June 1953), 116–33 and W. T. Waugh, 'The Great Statute of Praemunire' in *Eng. Hist. Rev.* (1922), 173–205.

THE PROGRESS OF PILGRIMAGE

Henry V was at Walsingham in 1421 during his last visit to England[1] and in 1427 Queen Joan came to St Albans after visits to Walsingham, Norwich and Peterborough;[2] the chronicler who notes her visit affords an interesting sidelight on the popularity of the shrine when he notes that, after Easter 1431, there was a fire at Little Walsingham which destroyed four inns there and was rumoured to have been started by pilgrims who had been charged extortionate prices.[3] About 1433 the pious Margery Kemp went to Walsingham to 'offer in worship of Our Lady'.[4] Evidently in 1456 and 1457 the abbot of Peterborough came here on pilgrimage, paying 20s. for his expenses on each occasion.[5]

The year 1455 had seen 'the duc of Yorke...beyng comme out of Irlande ridynge to oure Lady of Walsyngham in pylgrymage'[6] Henry VI visited Walsingham in 1447, 1448 and 1459,[7] and on 18 November 1456 Sir John Fastolf wrote to John Paston, 'my Lord of Norffolk is remevid from Framlyngham on foote to goo to Walsyngham'.[8] In 1460, Warwick the kingmaker was on pilgrimage here with his wife.[9] In October of the next year it was rumoured the king was going to Walsingham.[10] In 1465 Edward IV certainly licensed the priory to acquire in mortmain lands and rents to the considerable value of £40 yearly 'that they may pray

[1] J. H. Wylie and W. T. Waugh, *The Reign of Henry the Fifth* (1929), III, 272.
[2] J. Amundesham, *Chronicon* (R.S. 28), I, 26.   [3] *Ibid.* 62.
[4] *The Book of Margery Kempe*, ed. W. Butler Bowdon (1936), 310, 378.
[5] *The Book of William Morton*, ed. W. T. Mellows, P. I. King and C. N. L Brooke (1954), 86, 106; I owe this reference to Mr Brooke.
[6] *C.C.R.* (*1454–61*), 77.
[7] M. E. Christie, *Henry VI* (1922), 382, 384–5.
[8] *The Paston Letters*, ed. J. Gairdner (4 vols. 1900), I, 411.
[9] Jehan de Waurin, *Recueil des Croniques* (R.S. 39), V, 309.
[10] *Paston Letters*, II, 54.

EARLY BEQUESTS TO THE SHRINE

for the good estate of the king and Elizabeth his queen and for the king's soul after death'[1] and in 1469 the royal pair were evidently at Walsingham,[2] whilst the king was expected there again in October 1475,[3] after absence in France, as was the duke of Buckingham three years later.[4]

As usual the lower orders left little or no trace of their visits but there must have been not a few who turned their eyes to Our Lady of Walsingham in their hour of need. When John Paston developed a 'grete dysese', his wife 'be hestyd to gon on pylgreymmays to Walsingham', whilst his mother-in-law 'be hestyd a nodyr ymmage of wax of the weytte of yow to oyer Lady of Walsyngham'[5] (September 1443). The cost of a pilgrimage from Ghent to Our Lady of Walsingham was estimated at four livres.[6]

By this time medieval wills provide further signs of the popularity of the shrine. But the accessions from this source were not numerous, to judge by surviving evidence; and it is clear that most of the offerings at the shrine were made by pilgrims at the time of their visit, though a few made arrangements for another to carry out a posthumous pilgrimage for them. One of the earliest gifts bequeathed to the shrine, of which knowledge has survived, is that made in 1326 by Archbishop Walter Reynolds of Canterbury, who left altar ornaments and fittings to the shrine of Our Lady of Walsingham.[7] In 1367 one Sir Thomas Uvedale left to the

[1] *C.P.R.* (*1461–7*), 484–5. [2] *Paston Letters*, II, 353–4, 355.
[3] *Ibid.* III, 141.   [4] *Ibid.* III, 234.   [5] *Ibid.* I, 48.
[6] Waterton, *Pietas Mariana Britannica* (1879), 173 quoting Cannaert, *Witten Bouc*, 354.
[7] Hist. MSS. Rep., 5th Rep., App. 460.
H. P. Feasey (*Our Ladye of Walsingham*, Weston-super-Mare, 1901, p. 23) notes a bequest in 1317 by Gilbert Russell for pilgrimages to Compostella, Rocamadour, Bromholm, Walsingham and Canterbury.

chapel at Walsingham a silver tablet gilt with the salutation of the Blessed Virgin, together with a painted image,[1] and 10 marks to the building of the choir.[2] Twenty years before, John earl of Surrey had bequeathed 'mon egle dez saune les anels qe sount mys par constellation'.[3] In 1369 Sir Bartholomew Burghersh, a founder of the order of the Garter, left 'my body to be buried in the chapel of Walsyngham before the image of the Blessed Virgin'[4] which implies some sort of offering, and in 1381 William earl of Suffolk willed a statuette of a horse and man armed with his arms to be made in silver and 'offered to the altar of Our Lady of Walsingham'.[5] The previous year Edmund earl of March had devised to the house forty marks and an elaborate set of white vestments and altar furnishings.[6]

By her will, proved in 1360, Elizabeth de Burgh, Lady Clare, patron of the priory, bequeathed to it £4 in pence, two cloths of gold and a silver and enamel cup (*godet*) with a *trepar*.[7] In 1414 Semari de Tonge a baron of the Cinque Ports left 20 marks for masses in Our Lady's chapel before the image.[8] In 1433 Benedict, bishop of St David's, left £10 for various pilgrimages

---

[1] *Surrey Arch. Coll.* III, 151: 'unam tabellam argenteam et deauratam de Salutatione beatae Mariae cum una ymagine depicta'.
[2] Below, 76.
[3] *Testamenta Eboracensia* (Surtees Soc.), I, 41.
[4] *Testamenta Vetusta* (ed. N. H. Nicholas, 2 vols., 1826), I, 77.
[5] *Ibid.* 115.
[6] *Royal Wills* (ed. J. Nichols, 1780), 107, 109; '...une chapelle blanche, cest assavoir, deuz curtynes, trois aubes, trois amytes, deux estoles, trois fanons, un chesible, deux tonicles, trois chapes, deux fronteles, un towaill ove un frountell, un longe towaill pur l'autier, un cas pour un corporas avec le corporas acordant a la chapele, toute d'une seute'.
[7] *Ibid.* 32. She had incurred the displeasure of the canons by founding a Franciscan friary at Walsingham. The text of their long and interesting petition against this step survives (see above, 26).
[8] *Register of Henry Chichele* (ed. E. F. Jacob, 3 vols.), II (1937), 13.

including one to Walsingham, to be made 'with all possible haste'[1] ('cum festinacione possibili') after his death, whilst the same year Thomas, bishop of Worcester, bequeathed a share of 'all my relics which I brought from Rome in two small bags'.[2] The will of Isabel, countess of Warwick (1440) provided that 'my tablet with the image of Our Lady, having a glass for it, be offered to Our Lady of Walsyngham as also my gown of green alyz cloth of gold with wide sleeves, and a tabernacle in silver like in the timber to that over Our Lady of Caversham'.[3] In 1471 William Ponte bequeathed 6s. 8d. to the shrine and 1s. to 'any of those who will pilgrimage for me to Blessed Marye of Walsingham',[4] and in 1474 Lady Elizabeth Andrew bequeathed a ring with diamonds.[5] In 1483 Anthony Wydevill, Earl Rivers, bequeathed his 'trapper of blakk cloth of gold'.[6]

The large number of published North country wills suggests that Walsingham had comparatively little attraction there, partly, perhaps, because of the great repute of Saint Cuthbert, partly also because of that isolationist spirit of the land north of the Humber which was so marked throughout the Middle Ages. But in 1453 Lord John Scrope of Masham left 10 marks for 'forgeten avowes and beheestes' made by him to Our Lady of Walsingham.[7] In 1472 the will of William Ecopp, of Heslerton, ordained that after his death a pilgrim or pilgrims should go on his behalf, *inter alia*, to Walsingham and six other sanctuaries of Our Lady offering 4d. at each.[8] In 1498 William Mauleverer left the house 'a

[1] *Ibid.* 485. [2] *Ibid.* 491.
[3] *Testamenta Vetusta*, I, 240. [4] *Ibid.* 326. [5] *Ibid.* 329.
[6] S. Bentley, *Excerpta Historica* (1831), 248.
[7] *Testamenta Eboracensia* (Surtees Soc.), II, 192.
[8] *Ibid.* III, 201.

litell ring with a diamount, that king Richard gave me',[1] and Lady Ann Scrope left 'x of my grete beedes lassed with sylke crymmesyn and goold with a grete botton of goold and tasselyd with the same'.[2] In 1505 Lady Catherine widow of Sir John Hastings bequeathed to Walsingham her velvet gown.[3]

Although a great number of medieval wills have not been examined, the above bequests to Walsingham are all to be found among several thousand consulted by the writer. It is, indeed, clear from the most cursory study of these that the habit of making bequests to far distant good causes is a very modern one. The mass of charitable bequests were to very local institutions, notably, of course, the testator's parish church, and the few of wider importance seem to have been due to some private devotion or to special reasons, such as that which led the nobility to make gifts to religious houses of which they were patrons. Certainly there is little doubt that only a very small part of Walsingham's wealth came from bequests.

Infinitely more important was the wealth derived from offerings made at the shrine by those on pilgrimage there. Unhappily we have but the scantiest evidences of these. The only account roll from the priory traced by the writer is one of the cellarer for the year 1495–6,[4] which, however, does not deal with this side of the revenue. The chronicler John Capgrave quotes from some annals of the chapel of Walsingham which contained, *inter alia*, details of some important gifts to the shrine. Henry, duke of Lancaster (d. 1361), he tells us,

---

[1] *Testamenta Eboracensia*, IV, 182 n.   [2] *Ibid.* IV, 153.   [3] *Ibid.* IV, 257.
[4] Society of Antiquaries of London, MS. 622: 'Compotus domini Thome Bynham in officio cellerarii' (10–11 Hen. VII). Some short, quite minor accounts not connected with the shrine survive on the flyleaves of a Bible from the priory (see below, 115).

gave a cup and other things to the total value of about 400 marks, whilst his father Henry, earl of Lancaster, gave what was evidently a picture of the Annunciation with precious stones also of an estimated value of 400 marks[1]—the disappearance of this manuscript is, perhaps, more to be regretted than that of any other belonging to the priory. Under such circumstances we are forced to rely principally on the very few donors' accounts which have survived to get glimpses of the offerings made at the shrine.

Inevitably most of these are accounts of the royal household, and the gifts they record are inevitably much more lavish than was usual with donors of less degree. The gifts of Henry III have already been noted. Various benefactions of Edward have been found. The king had £14. 15s. 2d. of silver given to William de Fardon 'from which to make an image in the likeness of the lord king' and also 2½ ounces of gold 'for gilding the same image which was offered in the chapel of blessed Mary at Walsingham'.[2] The Account Roll of 18 Edward I shows that on 8 February the king made offerings of 7s. each 'at the statue of Blessed Mary in the small chapel of Walsingham' and 'at the statue of the blessed Gabriel in the same chapel'.[3] The roll of 28 Edward I records some most valuable and extensive particulars of royal offerings. On 15 May 1300, the king offered 7s. and a gold brooch (*firmaculum*) valued at 8 marks 'at the statue of Blessed Mary in the chapel of Walsingham' and 7s. each 'at relics placed above the same altar' and 'at the statue of Saint Gabriel and the

[1] 'Salutationem angelicam cum lapidibus pretiosis', *Liber de illustribus Henricis* (R.S. 7), 164.

[2] P.R.O., Wardrobe Accounts, E. 352, no. 84 m. 1 (22 March 1282 to 20 November 1284); I owe this reference to Mr A. J. Taylor.

[3] P.R.O., Chan. Misc., 46, m. 1.

lac beate Marie at the high altar in the priory church there'. On behalf of the queen, 7*s*. and a gold brooch valued at 6½ marks were offered in Our Lady's chapel and 7*s*. at 'the milk of blessed Mary in the church of the aforesaid priory'. Whilst ten days later (25 May) 'the Lord Edward' (the future King Edward II) offered a shilling at the high altar and 7*s*. at the altar in the chapel of Our Lady.[1] Two years later, on 30 March, the same stock payment of 7*s*. was made by the king at the altar of the chapel and at the high altar of the priory church.[2] On 6 October 1315, seven shillings was given on behalf of King Edward II (then at the priory) 'at various relics in the chapel of blessed Mary of Walsingham'. The queen gave the same amount 'at the altar in the small chapel' of the priory and a gold brooch set with stones costing 40*s*.[3]

Edward III, on the first visit of his reign to Walsingham (20 September 1328) made gifts at the altar in Our Lady's chapel and to the statue of Our Lady there, to a total value of 83*s*. 4*d*., which included valuable cloth and a gold brooch with jewels.[4]

Such offerings as this give us some idea of the way in which the wealth of Walsingham steadily increased in the fourteenth and fifteenth centuries. By the end of the period it was clearly getting a big part of its revenue from these offerings and was in a position to invest considerable sums in land. In 1425 the priory got a licence to acquire considerable Norfolk property for which privilege the king was paid 100 marks,[5] another

---

[1] *Liber quotidianus contrarotulatoris garderobae anno 28 Edwardi primi* (Soc. of Antiquaries, 1787), 36, 39, 334.
[2] P.R.O., E. 101/361/13, m. 2.
[3] P.R.O., E. 101/376/7, mm. 4, 5, 9.
[4] P.R.O., E. 101/383/14.
[5] *C.P.R.* (*1422–9*), 270.

for £100 in 1448,[1] followed by a grant in mortmain for £10 in 1453,[2] another licence for £40 annual value in 1465[3] and one for £24 in 1481.[4] A final considerable indication of the financial resources of Walsingham at this time is provided by the great list of properties acquired by Prior John Farewell[5] (1474–1503), for which he paid the gigantic sum of £717. 5s. 6d.

Published materials for Tudor history are substantially more ample than those for preceding generations, and leave no shadow of doubt as to the enormous repute of the shrine in its last days. Nowhere is there any effective evidence of any decline in the popularity of Walsingham[6] and there is much to show that it continued highly attractive.

The shrine at this time seems to have had no greater devotee than Henry VII. Polydore Vergil tells us how, in the crisis of 1487 when his throne was in grave peril, Henry 'came to the place called Walsingham where he prayed devoutly before the image of the Blessed Virgin

[1] *Ibid.* (*1446–52*), 180. [2] *Ibid.* (*1452–61*), 68.
[3] *Ibid.* (*1461–7*), 484–5.
[4] *Ibid.* (*1476–85*), 223 (in part satisfaction of a previous licence).
[5] Cartul. fo. 59ᵛ = *Mon.* 75 where the list is given in full.
[6] Only two allegations to this effect have been noted, both of which are suspect. In a big licence to alienate in mortmain, granted by Henry VI in 1448, it is asserted that the house 'is so poorly endowed that the profits of their possessions scarce suffice to celebrate divine service' (*C.P.R.* (*1446–52*), 180), but this is nothing more than a stock chancery formula used in a place where it is utterly inappropriate. The wealth of Walsingham is adequately proved by the Valor Ecclesiasticus of 1535 (below, 59–60) when half of its income came from endowments, and from the note in the cartulary of its wealth in the time of Prior Farewell just noted. Wolsey's grant of Flitcham priory to Walsingham in 1528 asserts that 'the universal devotion by which it [Walsingham] was first sustained is now cooled by the perverse reviling of some and the pestiferous preaching of others' (*L. and P.* IV, no. 2254); but the other contemporary evidence does not support this, which, again, is probably a purely conventional phrase aimed at providing a formal motive for the grant.

Mary (who is worshipped with special devotion there), that he might be preserved from the wiles of his enemies'.[1] And after the defeat of his rival, Lambert Simnel, the king sent Christopher Urswick with the military standard which he had used against the enemy whom he had defeated, to Walsingham, 'to offer thanks for the victory in the shrine of the Blessed Virgin and to place the standard there as a memorial of the favour he had received from God'.[2] On 7 March 1489, William Paston wrote that the king was expected to be at Norwich on Palm Sunday 'and so tary there all Ester, and than to Walsyngham',[3] and on 23 August 1498 Henry was there again.[4] On 16 April 1506 'the king toke his pilgrimage toward our Lady of Walsingham and the xxii day of the said moneth his hygnesse came to Cambrig'.[5] It was perhaps on this occasion that he offered at the shrine that 'ymage of silver and gilt...that we have caused to bee made to be offred and sette before our Lady at Walsingham' referred to in his will.[6] In 1502–3, the expenses of Elizabeth of York, aunt of the king, included numerous small donations to shrines, the largest being half a mark each to Our Lady of Walsingham and Our Lady of Sudbury.[7]

More surprising to many will be the evident devotion of Henry VIII to Our Lady of Walsingham in the early

[1] *Anglica Historia* ed. D. Hay, Camden Soc. LXXIV (1950), 21. Henry was apparently at Walsingham on 17 April 1487 (*Materials for the reign of Henry VII* (R.S. 60), II, 137).

[2] *Anglic. Hist.* 25; cf. J. Hardyng, *Chron.* (1812), 557, 'He incontynently sent his banner to Walsyngham to be consecrate to our Lady there to bee kepte for a perpetuall monument of victorie.'

[3] *Paston Letters*, III, 351.

[4] *Excerpta Hist.* (ed. S. Bentley), 119.

[5] Bodl. Lib. Oxf. MS. Ashmole 1113, fo. 126.

[6] T. Astle, *The Will of King Henry VII* (London, 1775), 37; the will fetches out very strongly the king's devotion to Our Lady.

[7] *Privy Purse Expenses of Elizabeth of York* (ed. N. H. Nicolas, 1830), 3.

years of his reign, a devotion which, one may suspect, was intimately bound up with his passionate desire for a son and heir. In Spelman's day men still told of Henry's pilgrimage to the shrine, when he walked barefoot to the shrine and offered to Our Lady a necklace of great value;[1] on what occasion this was we cannot be certain, but it must have been early in the reign. The king is known to have endowed a candle there. An annual payment of 46s. 8d. for this appears in 1509, 1510 and 1515,[2] which gift may have been made during a royal visit. In the accounts for 1525–6, 43s. 4d. was paid for the king's candle before Our Lady of Walsingham[3] and in 1529 the same sum appears.[4] There is also evidence of a sum of £10 yearly paid for a priest 'singing before Our Lady of Walsingham',[5] which continues down to the suppression of the shrine in 1538, which seems to be a quite recent obligation, though the Valor Ecclesiasticus of 1535 records that one had been established for the souls of Edward I and Edward II.[6] The payment of £1. 13s. 4d. made in January 1511[7] is described as 'offerings at Our Lady of Walsingham' and presumably followed the birth of the young Prince Henry on New Year's Day, 1511; certainly before the queen had been churched the king hurried off to Walsingham,[8] evidently to give

[1] 'Obtinuit fama celebris me adhuc puero, Regem Angliae Henricum VIII nudis pedibus a Bashamia [Barsham] ad praesentiam Virginis perrexisse, conceptisque votis monile peringentis pretii obtulisse,' *Reliquiae Spelmanniane* (ed. E. Gibson, 1723), II, 149. For another reference to barefooted pilgrimage to Walsingham see *L. and P.* VII, 454.

[2] *Ibid.* II (2), pp. 1442, 1445, 1469.

[3] B.M., Egerton MS. 2604, fo. 5ᵛ.   [4] *L. and P.* V, 309.

[5] *Ibid.* II (2), pp. 1442, 1445, 1469; V, p. 309; III (2), 1535; B.M., Egerton MS. 2604, fo. 5ᵛ.

[6] *Valor Ecclesiasticus* (Rec. Com.), III, 386; below, 60.

[7] *L. and P.* II (2), 1449. A royal grant of 23 September 1513 is dated at Walsingham (*ibid.* I (2), no. 2422 (2)) when Henry was abroad.

[8] E. Hall, *Chronicle* (1809 ed.), 517.

thanks. Much more significant are the two payments totalling £43. 11s. 4d. made to Barnard Flower in 1511-12 for glazing the Lady chapel at Walsingham.[1] Barnard was the royal glazier, to become famous for his work at King's College Chapel, Cambridge, and it is highly likely that this commission to him was in the nature of a thank-offering or (in view of the early death of the prince) of a continued plea for divine aid. That Queen Katherine was party to this invocation of the aid of Our Lady of Walsingham in the momentous matter of a male heir to the throne is perhaps hinted at in the pathetic postscript to her letter to Henry of 16 September 1513, announcing the great victory over the Scots at Flodden Field—'And with this I make an ende, praying God to sende you home shortly, for without this noo joye here can bee accomplisshed; and for the same I pray and now goo to Our Lady at Walsyngham that I promised soo long agoo to see'.[2] In March 1517 she was there again.[3] Amongst the lands granted to the queen were the manors of Great and Little Walsingham[4] and Katherine's will (1536) provided 'that some personage go to Our Lady of Walsingham on pilgrimage and distribute 20 nobles on the way'.[5] In 1524 Wolsey had secured a brief of plenary indulgence for the king and queen if they would make an annual pilgrimage to Walsingham, Bury St Edmunds or Canterbury with power to name twenty other persons to partake of it.[6]

[1] *L. and P.* II (2), 1451, 1458.
[2] H. Ellis, *Original Letters illustrative of English History* (1834), I, 89 (= *L. and P.* I (2), no. 2268). The queen was evidently at Walsingham on 23 September (*ibid.* 2422 (2)).
[3] *Ibid.* II (2), no. 3018.
[4] *Ibid.* II (2), no. 3893. (In 1495 these had been assigned in jointure to Queen Elizabeth, *Rotuli Parliamentorum* (Rec. Com.), VI, 463a.)
[5] *L. and P.* X, no. 40.   [6] *Ibid.* IV, no. 652.

TUDOR PILGRIMS AND BEQUESTS

Some years earlier—in 1514—a most interesting letter from Sir Edward Howard to the king shows a similar devotion to Walsingham in 'Master Arthur' (Lord Lisle, illegitimate son of Edward IV). He was given liberty to go home on landing after a naval action off Brest 'for Sir when he was in extreme danger and hope gone from hym he called upon Our Lady of Walsingham for help and comfort and made a vow that, and it pleased God and her to deliver him owt off that peril, he would never eet fleshe nor fyche tyl he had seen heer. Sir I assure you he was in mervelous danger, for it was merveil that the shipp beyng under al her sayls strikyng full but a rok with her stam that she brake not on peces at the first strok.'[1]

Considering the sparsity of the evidence on this sort of point, even at this period, it is remarkable how many dignitaries are known to have visited or supported Walsingham in these days. Wolsey came early in September 1517 to fulfil a vow 'and also to take air and exercise which may correct the weakness of his stomach'[2] and again in 1520.[3] Bishop West of Ely revived 'the old complaint in his leg' when riding to Walsingham in 1523[4] and in 1519 the duke of Buckingham vicariously offered half a mark at the shrine.[5] The marquis of Exeter's accounts for 1525 show that while spending 3*d.* on cherries for himself and his lady and expending 20*s.* 6*d.* at cards, he contrived to contribute 4*d.* to the

---

[1] *L. and P.* I, no. 1786.
[2] *Ibid.* II (2), nos. 3655, 3676, and appendix no. 38.
[3] *Ibid.* III (1), nos. 894, 1113.
[4] *Ibid.* III (2), no. 3476.
[5] *Ibid.* III (1), p. 499. *The Northumberland Household Book (1512)* (London, 1770), 252, shows that the duke of Northumberland was paying for the maintenance of a candle 'birnynge yerly befor Our Lady of Walsyngham' and sending a yearly offering of 4*d.*

shrine.[1] In June 1528 Bishop Tunstall of London wrote to Wolsey that he had 'promised a pilgrimage to Walsingham'[2] as had Bishop Longland of Lincoln 'as sone as my strengthe will serve me,'[3] though a baker and a friend from Colchester said it was idolatrous to do this at Walsingham, Ipswich or elsewhere.[4] Amongst lesser folk one John Haly wrote early in 1531 of his intention to visit Walsingham and Cambridge and so return to Warwickshire;[5] and in the following year John Beyston, a servant of the prior of Spalding, made a pilgrimage to Walsingham 'by order of his mother'.[6] Late in 1536 we hear of 'some Cornish soldiers who were coming from the North on a pilgrimage to Walsingham',[7] and amongst the last to see the shrine in its full glory was Thomas O'Reef, an Irish priest dismissed by the archbishop of Dublin for 'popishness', whose presence at Walsingham is mentioned in 1538.[8] The Lincoln wills for the years 1516–32 contain fourteen bequests to Our Lady of Walsingham from people of no great social importance. All but two of these are small sums of money, 4*d.* being the usual sum though one was 6*d.*, one 8*d.*, and two 1*s.*;[9] of the other two cases, Richard Smyth left money for 'iij messys before Our Lady of Walsynghan, continuyng the space of iii yeres',[10] whilst Catherine Barton bequeathed 'a corse gyrdell with a pendyll and a bukkyl of sylver'.[11] Amongst the other humbler gifts at this time were the 'corall bedys of

[1] *L. and P.* IV, p. 794.   [2] *Ibid.* IV (2) no. 4418.
[3] H. Ellis, *Original Letters...*, 3rd Series (1846), I, 252.
[4] *L. and P.* IV (2), no. 4175; for another reference to the practice, see *ibid.* no. 4545.
[5] *Ibid.* V, no. 530.   [6] *Ibid.* V, no. 1576.
[7] *Ibid.* XI, no. 1260.   [8] *Ibid.* XIII (1), no. 1478.
[9] *Lincoln Wills* (ed. C. W. Foster), I, 73, 126, 143; II, 82; III, 14, 30, 32, 102, 115, 162, 183, 200.
[10] *Ibid.* II, 148.   [11] *Ibid.* III, 77.

thrys fyfty and my maryeng ryng with all thyngys hangyng theron' bequeathed in 1504 by Anne Barett of Bury.[1] The will of Sir Roger Strange of February 1505–6 left £26. 13s. 4d. 'to be paid to a prest for to synge for me and my frendys beforne our lady att Walsyngham during the tyme of iiij years'.[2]

Amongst the distinguished foreigners who visited Walsingham at this time the most famous was Desiderius Erasmus. On 9 May 1512, he writes of his having taken a vow to go to Walsingham and hang a Greek ode there.[3] It is thought that he went there soon afterwards and it is possible, though not certain, that he paid a second visit in 1514.[4] In the 1526 edition of his *Colloquies* first appeared his rather misleading essay *Peregrinatio religionis ergo*[5] which has a longish account of his visit there. The light this throws on the shrine will be considered below.[6] In 1534 the imperial ambassador, Chapuys, had intended to go on pilgrimage to Walsingham, but had given up the project as 'it would be thought I had gone chiefly to visit the Queen',[7] who was evidently residing nearby.

---

[1] *Wills and Inventories from Bury St Edmund's* (ed. S. Tymms, Camden Soc. 1850), 98.
[2] *Norf. Arch.* IX, 235.
[3] *L. and P.* I (I), no. 1188 (= *Erasmi Epistolae*, ed. P. S. Allen, I, no. 262).
[4] *Ibid.* note.
[5] Preserved Smith, *A Key to the Colloquies of Erasmus* (Harvard Theol. Studies, XIII, 1927), 40–1.
[6] Pp. 53–8.   [7] *L. and P.* VII, p. 387.

CHAPTER III

THE LAST DAYS

In the last stages of its history, Walsingham swallowed up a few of the petty houses of the Austin canons whose strength was insufficient to maintain an effective existence.[1] Fourteenth-century plagues and floods had evidently severely sapped the strength of the little house at Peterstone. In 1440 the only religious left was the prior, then seventy-five years old, so a commission which included the prior of Walsingham was appointed to investigate the desirability of annexing it to Creake Abbey.[2] But Creake itself was probably not too strong and in 1449 Peterstone was made a cell of Walsingham.[3] Sixty years later, on 4 August 1509, with episcopal approval, Thomas, prior of Mountjoy, demised to the prior of Walsingham his house and lands for ten years subject to certain conditions for his own maintenance, including the provision of 'mete and drink and a servant to wait uppon hym as a gentleman haught to have'.[4] On Wolsey's fall Mountjoy was seized by its patron as an escheat.[5] Just before this happened—in 1528—Wolsey used his legatine powers to grant the priory of St Mary ad Fontes, Flitcham, which had fallen into decay, to Walsingham whose possessions it adjoined. But as four resident canons were to be maintained for

---
[1] On these see J. C. Dickinson, 'Early Suppressions of English Houses of Austin Canons' in *Medieval Studies presented to Rose Graham*, ed. V. Ruffer and A. J. Taylor (1950), 54–77.
[2] *C.P.R.* VIII, 78.
[3] J. C. Dickinson, *loc. cit.* 62; *C.P.R.* (*1446–52*), 297.
[4] *Cal. Anc. Deeds*, III, 258 (A 6056).
[5] F. Blomefield, *History of Norfolk* (1808), VIII, 231.

THE SIZE OF THE CONVENT

the celebration of divine service, a yearly pension of 10*s*. was to be paid to the bishop and a daily mass to be said for Wolsey,[1] it can have brought Walsingham little advantage.

It is much to be regretted that reports of the bishop's visitations for the medieval monasteries of Norwich diocese are almost all lost, apart from those for the half century before the Dissolution.[2] If there were any major disorders in the earlier centuries of the house's history, one might have expected some echo of it in the royal and papal records, but, so far, the only serious trouble found is that concerning John Snoring, already noted.[3]

Certain general factors should be noted which made the situation of Walsingham, as of other religious houses, difficult. It is now almost certain that the Black Death and its after-effects had the catastrophic result of reducing the monastic population of medieval England by some two-fifths.[4] At Walsingham this caused an immediate minor crisis which in 1364 led to the prior being allowed to dispense with four of his canons to be ordained priest provided they had completed their twenty-second year, in view of the shortage caused by the pestilence.[5] But the big drop in numbers here, as elsewhere, does not

---

[1] *L. and P.* IV (2), no. 5129.

[2] *Visitations of the Diocese of Norwich, 1492–1532*, ed. A. Jessop (Camden Soc. 1888); the earlier visitations have evidently perished. The very fine, surviving, medieval episcopal registers of Norwich deal almost entirely with other matters.

[3] In 1327 Walter prior of Walsingham and others were accused of housebreaking but it is not known whether the charge was justified; *C.P.R.* (*1327–30*), 214. At the end of the century there was trouble with Thomas Houlot of Fornsete, a canon who apostatized after theft, see *C. Pap. Reg.* IV, 502; he is also described as 'monk of Binham', *C.P.R.* (*1401–5*), 386.

[4] D. Knowles and R. Neville Hadcock, *Medieval Religious Houses of England and Wales* (1953), 54–5, 364–5.

[5] *C. Pap. Reg.* IV, 41.

THE LAST DAYS

seem to have been permanent, and the last visitations show a reasonable number of brethren. There were twenty canons in 1377[1] (which was perhaps almost as many as before the Black Death),[2] seventeen in 1494, twenty-five in 1514, twenty-three in 1532[3] (including four canons from the late priory of Flitcham) and twenty-two in 1534.[4]

Owing to the absence of the Norwich episcopal visitations before the late fifteenth century, little can safely be said about the internal life of the priory before this date. The over-luxuriance of the monastic revival in East Anglia after the Conquest had made life difficult for small houses in this area in later times, six of the Norfolk houses of the order being extinct before 1536.[5] But Walsingham's superior resources may well have helped to maintain a higher standard there and the cartulary list of canons[6] certainly shows that, in the hundred and fifty years before the suppression, Walsingham supplied priors to several small neighbouring houses of the order.[7]

It is further worthy of note that the educational level of East Anglian monastic life was evidently well below what was desired. The Norwich episcopal visitations edited by Jessop show a very remarkable number of monasteries lamenting the lack of a schoolmaster.[8] Walsingham, as an exceptionally wealthy house, was normally able to afford to send some of its brighter

---

[1] J. Cox Russell in *Traditio*, II (1944), 200, cited by Knowles and Hadcock, *op cit.* 157.
[2] *Ibid.*
[3] *Norwich Visitations*, 59, 113–22, 314.
[4] Below, 59.
[5] *V.C.H. Norfolk*, II, *passim*; six of fourteen houses of Austin canons in Suffolk had similarly failed to survive.
[6] Below, Appendix III.
[7] *Ibid.*
[8] *Norwich Visitations*, 19, 28, 59, 61, 77, 107, 125, 137–8, 165, 221.

members to the university,[1] but this did not solve the educational problems of the mediocre many, and at the visitation of 1494 Brother Alan Aylesham reported that 'the brethren have no schoolmaster in the house to teach them grammar'.[2] This suggests that most of the brethren had little learning before entering the house, and the cartulary list of names shows that, in fact, an overwhelming proportion of them came from petty Norfolk villages where schools are unlikely to have been found.

This visitation of 1494[3] is the first of its kind concerning Walsingham that is known to have survived. There appeared before the bishop the prior and sixteen canons. No very serious delinquency is revealed, unless we accept the unsupported allegation of Brother William Norwich that the prior refused to have him ordained priest and imprisoned him for several weeks, which may or may not be so. The other defects are few and of minor significance, tale-bearing, insolent servants, a prior prone to favouritism and brethren going outside the monastery without a companion.[4]

Nine years later, evidently in September 1503, died John Farewell[5] who was prior at the time of the visitation. His death led to a catastrophe in the history of the house which deserves considerable stress. One William Lowthe with the aid of those notorious government officials, Empson and Dudley, made himself prior by what looks like doubtful means. In July 1504 he received royal pardon for entering on temporalities without due

[1] *Ibid.* 253, cf. *Chapters of the Augustinian Canons* (ed. H. E. Salter, Oxford, 1922), 99.
[2] *Norwich Visitations*, 59.   [3] *Ibid.* 57–60.
[4] The bishop went on to order, *inter alia*, that accounts of the house should be kept by the cellarer and other officials regularly. The Society of Antiquaries' Account Roll of the cellarer of Walsingham for the year 1495–6 (above, 38) may well have been drawn up as a result of this.
[5] *C.P.R.* (*1494–1509*), 332.

THE LAST DAYS

acceptance,[1] and in 1514, on the petition of the canons, the king cancelled the *congé d'élire* of 19 Henry VII which, according to the canons, 'William Lowthe, Sir Richard Empson and Edmund Dudley on the death of Sir John Farewell unlawfully obtained, and upon which the said William Lowthe was elected prior'.[2]

The future showed only too clearly the disastrous effects of this elevation to the priorate of a man who was entirely unsuited for such responsibility. The visitation of 14 July 1514[3] was a very full one doubtless because of disturbing signs of unrest. The prior had clearly made most monstrous threats to the brethren against their making due revelations to the bishop, had appropriated revenues and property of the house including jewels from the chapel, and was accused of consorting with the wife of John Smith to whom he accorded various improper privileges. That Prior Lowthe was mentally deranged is suggested by the accusation that he kept an old fool ('senem fatuum') whom he compelled to wear a surplice and to go in public procession, and ordered to be given Holy Communion, that he made a canon who called Smith's wife a whore beg her pardon in the chapter house, that he struck a servant so violently that he died of the after-effects, and that he threatened to build prisons for ten of the brethren.

Inevitably under such a superior the common life had sadly decayed. It was reported that there were dissensions among the brethren, that some were slack in performing divine service and three or four were leading

---

[1] *C.P.R.* (*1494–1509*), 366.

[2] *L. and P.* 1 (2), no. 3408 (28). The prior and convent claimed that they had the right of free election.

[3] *Norwich Visitations*, 113–23.

a dissolute life drinking outside the monastery. The bishop evidently temporized. Lowthe was allowed to continue as prior, though he was not to punish brethren without certain safeguards, notably the approval of the prior of West Acre, who was also to see that Lowthe tendered proper accounts of the priory's finances; moreover two servants, one of them being John Smith (the other presumably his wife), were to be deported from Walsingham forthwith. However, a month later (30 August 1514) the bishop issued further regulations[1] and the next day secured the resignation of William Lowthe.[2]

The canons of Walsingham were now enjoined to put away their previous divisions and bitterness; unnecessary conversation with seculars within the monastic precinct and archery outside it were forbidden, as was undue dallying in houses in the town. Precautions were to be taken to lock the door of the treasury with two locks, one to be kept by the prior, the other by a senior brother chosen by the convent; whilst the gold, silver, rings, jewels and other oblations at the chapel of Our Lady were to be enumerated and recorded weekly.

Thus ended perhaps the unhappiest era in the history of the priory and it is singularly unfortunate that it was during this period that Erasmus gathered at Walsingham materials for his remarks on the shrine which are so often quoted and so ill understood. His famous account[3]

[1] *Ibid.* 147–8.
[2] *Ibid.* 149. It was probably the necessity of making adequate financial provision for the retired prior, as promised in the deed of resignation, that led to Lowthe being made prior of West Acre (*Norwich Visitations*, 164–7); as might have been expected the results were none too happy (*ibid.*).
[3] For the text of the *Colloquy* I have used the Leipzig edition of 1829. A translation with useful notes is given in J. G. Nichols, *Pilgrimages to St Mary of Walsingham and St Thomas of Canterbury* (London, 1875), and is utilized hereafter for most quotations from the *Colloquy*.

has so often been accepted at its face value by those nurtured in the naïve traditions of Victorian liberalism, that it is necessary to point out that it can only be accepted with considerable reservations. As a critic Erasmus was neither well informed nor friendly. His own sensitive nature had clearly suffered from the foolish attempt to make him take the religious habit as a boy, and, like many distinguished foreigners in Cambridge since, he found the English climate and diet inconducive to real peace of mind; whilst it should further be remembered that the *Colloquy on Pilgrimage* is one of four published in 1526 which constitute the high-water mark of his attacks on the popular religion of his day.[1] His visit to Walsingham seems to have been of the briefest, his information about it acquired through an interpreter, and he was not immune from the contemporary readiness to confuse crudity and humour.

Certainly the more closely we examine his remarks on Walsingham the more obvious do their exaggeration and inaccuracy become. Thus he places Walsingham 'at the extreme coast of England to the North west [*sic*] at about three miles distance from the sea',[2] though it is a good five miles inland; he says that the priory 'has scarcely any other resources than from the bounty of the Virgin',[3] though by this time half its annual income came from endowments as the Valor Ecclesiasticus plainly showed;[4] whilst his claim that Walsingham 'is

[1] Cf. Preserved Smith, *A Key to the Colloquies of Erasmus*, 39: 'If one considers the Colloquies with reference to the amount of liberal religious instruction and anti-clerical doctrine contained in them, it is noticeable that they rise to a crescendo towards the middle years and then drop off again in a diminuendo. The high-water mark is certainly given by the edition of February 1526. Nowhere else did Erasmus so belabor the most lucrative abuses and the most popular superstitions as in the four new dialogues therein contained.'

[2] Nichols, 11.   [3] *Idem*, 12.   [4] Below, 60.

the most frequented place throughout all England, nor could you easily find in that island a man who ventures to reckon on prosperity unless he yearly salutes her [Our Lady] with some small offering according to his ability'[1] shows a most unclassical exaggeration.

There is plenty of evidence of somewhat superstitious practices in the Church of Erasmus's day, but his account of Walsingham herein cannot command complete confidence, since in at least one major instance he seems guilty of deliberate misrepresentation. He tells us that over 'the two wells' (which must be taken to be those mentioned in the Pynson ballad and still surviving) there was in his day a shed which was said to have been 'suddenly and miraculously brought thither from a great distance',[2] and goes on to stress the stupidity of the guide and his failure to recognize the essentially modern nature of the building.

This is one of the few of Erasmus's allegations which we can check by other evidence, and the result is not encouraging. The rather earlier Pynson ballad shows that it is perfectly true that there then existed at Walsingham a tradition of a miraculous transportation. But the edifice to which the ballad applies the tradition was not a modern shed moved as a whole 'a great distance', but the venerable chapel of Our Lady, then some four centuries old, which was said to have been moved, when in process of construction, a bare 200 feet.[3] The two accounts cannot possibly be harmonized and it is difficult to avoid the conclusion that Erasmus, out of a donnish desire to tell a good story, had grossly twisted the facts.

He also gives a circumstantial account[4] of how the priory had acquired a relic of the so-called Holy Milk of

[1] Nichols, 11.   [2] *Idem*, 18.   [3] Below, 127.   [4] Nichols, 25–7.

Blessed Mary (*lac sacrum beate Marie*). That this had originally come from the East, as he alleges, is likely enough; we find Barnwell Priory owning relics which its founder had acquired on the First Crusade,[1] and Bridlington priory being given a reliquary from Jerusalem.[2] But other details of its history as given by Erasmus have been shown to be inaccurate or unlikely, and it is at least possible that the inscription in the church from which Erasmus claims to have got them is misrepresented by him.[3] Good reason has been given to show that the relic itself, described by Erasmus as 'dried up—you would say it was ground chalk mixed with white of egg',[4] was not what a literal interpretation would make it out to be but was merely a scraping from the chalky 'Grotto of Our Lady's Milk' in Bethlehem, a favourite medieval souvenir.[5] How soon knowledge of the original nature of the relic tended to be generally forgotten and to what extent it was alive in Erasmus's England are questions on which the writer does not feel qualified to draw any conclusions, though one may well feel that herein Erasmus has at least put the worst interpretation on the facts.

It is because one cannot feel sure that Erasmus has not embellished his account of Walsingham in a rather unfair way, that one regrets so much the absence of evidence regarding the other spectacular stories he tells.

---

[1] *Liber memorandorum ecclesie de Bernewelle* (ed. J. W. Clark, 1907), 46–7.

[2] *Chartulary of Bridlington Priory* (ed. W. T. Lancaster), 11.

[3] E. Waterton, *Pietas Mariana Britannica* (1879), 198–9.

[4] Nichols, 20.

[5] Waterton, *op. cit.* 201–5. A traveller writing in 1553–5 notes: 'The pilgrims take pieces of the earth of this grotto for the use of women who have no milk.... Mothers who have no milk are in the habit of using fragments of rock and earth from this grotto', *A Spanish Franciscan's Narrative of a Journey to the Holy Land* (trans. H. C. Luke, London, 1927), pp. 69, 36; the editor notes that the practice still prevails (36 n.).

ERASMUS ON WALSINGHAM

Whether we believe his report that he was given a piece 'cut from a beam on which the Virgin Mother had been seen to rest'[1] or not, must depend entirely on our estimate of his character and that of popular religion at this time. Similarly, one cannot be certain whether or no Erasmus has touched up the story of the 'Knight's Door'. This name was, and is, given to a small postern on the north side of the precinct wall. According to the *Colloquy* it took this name from a knight on horseback who was closely pursued by his enemy and miraculously saved by commending his safety to the Virgin, so that 'on a sudden the man and horse were together within the precincts of the church, and the pursuer fruitlessly storming without'.[2] This much of the story is paralleled in Blomefield, whose account is partly taken from 'an old MS.'[3] which may be an independent source. Under this door was 'an iron grating allowing only a footman to pass' and Erasmus asserts that this was put up after the escape 'as it would not be proper that any horse should again tread the spot which the former horseman had consecrated to the Virgin'. This may be so, but it is at least feasible that the grating was originally there to prevent its use by any but pedestrians (likely enough, since it was a conveniently placed exit for pilgrims after visiting the shrine) and that the alleged miraculous escape merely arose through someone on horseback having contrived to enter through it. Again, it is difficult to feel any confidence in Erasmus's jibe that the alleged relics of the True Cross would together make a shipload of timber,[4] a remark perhaps not intended to be taken literally.

[1] Nichols, 32.   [2] *Idem*, 16.
[3] F. Blomefield, *History of Norfolk*, IX, 280.
[4] See the evidence cited by Waterton (*op. cit.* 206–9).

THE LAST DAYS

Of the brethren of the priory, as distinct from the cult there, Erasmus has little critical to say and that not of great importance. It is not easy to feel much amusement or concern at his somewhat snobbish references to the Walsingham canons' ignorance of Greek[1] (which they shared with all but the minutest fraction of contemporary western society), and their consequent failure to distinguish between Greek and Arabic in the case of his ode.[2] Nor can it be regarded as surprising or grossly reprehensible if several of the brethren, as Erasmus asserts, contrived to catch a glimpse of the distinguished visitor.[3] In any case Erasmus found fit to describe the convent as 'highly spoken of; richer in piety than in revenue'.[4]

Between the time of Erasmus's visit to Walsingham and the publication of his *Colloquy on Pilgrimages*, episcopal visitations were continuing, and give us valuable details on the conventual life at Walsingham. In July 1520 it is clear that the situation had improved though it was still far from perfect.[5] There were no grave scandals but the new prior was having difficulty in ruling a house divided against itself. There was dissension among the brethren; some refused to consent to the sealing of proxies to excuse the prior from attending 'the assembly of superiors summoned by the lord Cardinal' (that is, the general chapter for Austin canons called by Wolsey in 1519) and the consistory court of Norwich, whilst a number of the brethren refused to accept the new statutes. The refractory brethren were ordered to submit and ask pardon for their offence.

The next visitation[6] came at what was apparently the

[1] Nichols, 31–2.
[2] *Idem*, 28.
[3] *Idem*, 23, 29.
[4] *Idem*, 12.
[5] *Norwich Visitations*, 170–2.
[6] *Ibid.* 252–3.

THE LAST VISITATIONS

normal six-year interval (August 1526) and showed that the situation had again improved. Several brethren said that all was well and though others mentioned defects, none of these were of a serious nature. There was the old complaint that the young brethren had no one to teach them. It was said that the house had ceased to maintain a scholar at the university, whilst two brethren complained that the subprior was inclined to favouritism and severity. In 1529 the prior of Coxford made various complaints against the bishop of Norwich and the prior of Walsingham, though it is not known to what extent they were justified.[1] At the visitation of 1532[2] Walsingham was pleasingly peaceful. Most brethren said that all was well, the only dissenting voice being that of Brother William Race who maintained that the convent's attendance at mattins was irregular. There were at this time twenty-two brethren besides the prior, four of whom were novices and four ex-canons of Flitcham.

By now the first rumbles of the Reformation were beginning. On 18 September 1534, Prior Richard Vowell and twenty-one canons signed a deed accepting King Henry VIII as 'head of the English Church' and rejecting the authority of the pope.[3] In the following year was compiled the Valor Ecclesiasticus, the great valuation of the wealth of the English Church, which gives us most valuable details of Walsingham's financial resources. The gross general income of the priory was estimated at £707. 7s. 10½d. with a net value of

---

[1] *L. and P.* IV (3), no. 5511; the charges suggest an attempt to suppress the priory of Coxford.
[2] *Norwich Visitations*, 314–15.
[3] *L. and P.* VII, no. 1216 (27), printed in *Arch. Journ.* XIII (1856), 128–9.

£652. 4s. 11⅜d.[1] The lands owned by the priory were very extensive and almost all in Norfolk, the gross temporal income being £385. 0s. 0⅜d. The spiritual revenues were derived from two sources. The rectories of All Saints' in Great Walsingham and of St Peter's, and of All Saints' in Little Walsingham totalled £59. 10s. 5d. Much more valuable, more unusual and more interesting are the offerings at the shrine (*oblaciones*) which the Valor shows under three heads. Those at the relic of the so-called 'Holy Milk of the Blessed Mary the Virgin' amounted annually to only 42s. 3d., those 'in the chapel of St Laurence' to £8. 9s. ½d. for the same period; but those 'in the chapel of the Blessed Virgin Mary' totalled no less than £250. 1s.—more than the total income of many a medium-sized monastery.[2] There were annual payments for the maintenance of lights and 12s. 6d. for twenty-five poor at Bedingham, whilst 106s. 8d. was paid yearly to a chaplain celebrating divine service in the chapel of Our Lady for the souls of Edward I, Edward II, and John Uvedale, knight.[3] A chaplain was also paid 106s. 8d. to celebrate for the souls of John Marshall and his wife Ellen ('Alina').

In Harl. MS. 791 are preserved some curious Articles of Enquiry.[4] They are headed 'Walsingham' and consist of a series of very detailed questions regarding the value of the offerings at the shrine: whether these were inventoried or alienated or pledged; what relics were there and where these were exposed; whether miracles at the shrine were claimed and 'wonte to be declared in pulpite heretofore' and what proof there

[1] *Valor Ecclesiasticus* (Rec. Com.), III, 385–8.
[2] *Ibid.* III, 386. The offerings to the Holy Rood of Bromholm had now shrunk to a mere £5. 12s. 9d.
[3] See above, 43 and *Surrey Arch. Coll.* III, 71.
[4] Fos. 27r–28r; printed in Nichols, 209–12.

THE WEALTH OF THE SHRINE

was for such claims; what stories were told about the origin of the house and of the statue; 'whether our Ladye's milk be liquid or no' and 'what of the house where the bere skynne[1] is and of the knyght'. These articles are unfortunately undated but it has long been recognized that they have been influenced by Erasmus's account of Walsingham. The inquiry here envisaged evidently preceded the attack on images launched by the royal injunctions of August 1536, for before this date we have evidence of some intention to rob the shrine. As early as 25 July 1536, a letter from one of his agents to Thomas Cromwell reported that all the money, plate and jewels at Walsingham had been sequestered,[2] a step probably contemplated before October 1535.[3] It is difficult to see what justification there could be for this act at this stage. The Act suppressing the smaller monasteries passed in February 1536 could not apply to Walsingham whose wealth put it high up among what the Act called 'great solemn monasteries wherein thanks be to God, religion is well kept and observed'. The letter adds the interesting note that 'frome the Satreday night tyll the Sondaye next folowinge was ofred at their now beinge 133s. 4d.' besides wax, and note that the visitors had found 'a secrete prevye place within the howse, where no channon nor annye other of the howse dyd ever enter, as they saye' and that among the implements there was 'nothing there wantinge that shoulde belonge to the arte of multyplyeng'. This

---

[1] The bearskin is mentioned by Erasmus. Waterton, *op. cit.* 319, shows it may have been used as a rug.

[2] *L. and P.* XI, no. 165; printed in full in T. Wright, *Letters relating to the Suppression of the Monasteries* (Camden Soc. 1843), 138–9, and Nichols, 213–14.

[3] A letter of the prior to Cromwell of October 1535 shows that a valuation of oblations was then under way (*L. and P.* IX, no. 678).

THE LAST DAYS

suggestion of false coining is in line with the behaviour of Cromwell's servants but it is at least as likely that the workshop in question was used for the manufacture of the pilgrim tokens which are known to have been on sale at this time.[1] It is worth noting in this connexion that a building for this purpose was found at Christchurch, Canterbury, England's other major pilgrimage centre.

At this time Walsingham like other religious houses of the diocese of Norwich suffered from a visitation by royal officials 'of doubtful character'[2] concerned to provide propaganda material for the total dissolution of monastic life in England. Their report, quite worthless as evidence, accused some canons of fleshly sins and the house of 'much superstition in feigned relics and miracles'.[3] In September 1536, Richard Vowell, the then prior of Walsingham, wrote to Cromwell an obscure letter about some mysterious domestic matter, saying that all his brethren 'deny that they were privy either to the articles or to the letter sent to Cromwell in their name' and adding that the bearer will deliver Cromwell's 'fee for the ensuing year'.[4]

That pilgrimages were still going on, however, is clear from the mention of a visit by Cornish soldiers at this time[5] and from a curious report of trouble at the shrine. On 3 June 1537, it was deposed that a priest

---

[1] It is just conceivable that the priory had rented some room within its precinct to a townsman who was uttering false coin, as Henry Capron mercer of Little Walsingham had done a little before (*L. and P.* IV (3), g. 6418 [27]). Prof. Dickins suggests the possibility that the place was being used for experiments in alchemy.

[2] J. R. Tanner, *Tudor Constitutional Documents, A.D. 1485–1603* (Cambridge, 1940), 58.

[3] *L. and P.* x, p. 143.

[4] *Ibid.* XI, 480; a list of fees monthly from monasteries about this time includes £4 from Walsingham, *ibid.* XI, appendix no. 16.

[5] Above, 46.

at Our Lady's chapel 'on Our Lady's Even before Christmas' had said to four men of Lincolnshire who came on pilgrimage to Walsingham that 'if Norfolk and Suffolk would have risen when Lincolnshire and Yorkshire did, they had been able to have gone through the realm'. This was a reference to the Pilgrimage of Grace, a rising recently inspired by the suppression of the smaller monasteries, but the accusation of disloyalty was clearly suspect as it came from a 'soore and diseased beggar' whose importunity at the chapel door had so irritated pilgrims that they invoked the aid of the priest. The beggar attacked him with 'froward and naughty words' for which a constable finally put him in the stocks, after which he made his accusation against the priest.[1] But there was bound to be much discontent at the dismantling of the monasteries now going on apace on every hand, not least in an area whose past was as inextricably involved with monasticism as Norfolk, and it is not surprising that a rising here was planned in which Walsingham was implicated.

In mid April 1537, one Ralph Rogerson meeting one George Gysburghe of Walsingham in the town had said to him, 'You see how these abbeys go down and our living goeth away with them; for within a while Bynham shall be put down and also Walsingham and all other abbeys in that country',[2] and had suggested opposition. The sequel was a plot to rebel, hatched under cover of a shooting match at Binham.[3] Those involved seem to have been few and were largely local laity of no great influence, but their efforts were enough to jolt

[1] *L. and P.* XII (2), no. 21.

[2] *Ibid.* XI (1), 1056. George Gysburghe was later accused of saying 'that he thought it very evil done the suppressing of so many religious houses where God was well served' and of suggesting insurrection.

[3] *Ibid.* XII (1), no. 1125.

THE LAST DAYS

a somewhat nervy government. Unhappily for the conspirators their plans were betrayed at an early stage by one John Galant of Letheringsett, a servant of Sir John Heydon who alleged that the conspirators 'aimed at 'raising the country' and going to the aid of 'the Northern men'.[1]

Sir John, a member of a well-established local family, stood firm by the government, and on 26 April 1537 wrote hastily of 'a great insurrection like to be among the King's subjects about Walsyngham.... Tonight or early in the morning I intend to be at Walsingham to apprehend some of these rebellious, and trust to hear from my lord how I shall act.'[2] But three days later Richard Southwell wrote to Cromwell that Heydon had informed him 'the conspirators do not pass 12 in numbers, all very beggars and there is no likelihood of any commotion'.[3] The rebels were sought out and on 3 May Cromwell was informed that the subprior of Walsingham (Nicholas Mileham) was 'infectyd' and had been taken and examined.[4] A week later, on 10 May 1537, Sir Roger Townsend and Richard Southwell acknowledged receipt of letters from the king and Cromwell, ordering the execution 'without sparing' of all offenders in the Walsingham conspiracy.[5] In pursuance of this, the subprior and George Gisborough, evidently a layman of the town, were drawn, hanged, beheaded and quartered at Walsingham on 30 May 1537, nine of their confederates suffering similarly at other places in Norfolk.[6]

Prior Richard Vowell evidently hoped against hope that his house would survive, but if it had not been

[1] *L. and P.* XII (1), no. 1045.   [2] *Ibid.* no. 1046.
[3] *Ibid.* no. 1063.   [4] *Ibid.* no. 1125.   [5] *Ibid.* no. 1171.
[6] *Ibid.* no. 1300, where a list of those executed is given.

THE END OF THE SHRINE

implicated in the abortive rising its wealth must have proved an irresistible temptation to the extravagant king, who by now had decided on the total suppression of monasteries in England. A short lull, however, followed. For some months after the executions little is known about the house till on 14 July 1538 we find the prior reporting to Cromwell that the royal commissioners had taken the image of Our Lady from the chapel 'allso all suche golde and syllver with such other thynges as weare theare,[1]' leaving in his keeping some silver. He went on to urge the expenses that the priory would be liable to incur by being unable to observe certain compulsory ecclesiastical obligations under the new conditions,[2] and continued to urge, as he had evidently done before,[3] 'the translacion of our house into a college'. On 18 July the image that for centuries had evoked so much piety reached London along with the statue of Our Lady of Ipswich and 'all the jewelles that hunge about them'.[4] Their fate was uncertain at this date.[5] A month earlier Latimer had written to Cromwell urging the burning of certain famous statues of Our Lady, including that of Walsingham,[6] and this course was decided on 'because the people should use noe more idolatrye unto them'.[7] They were destroyed at Chelsea probably before July was out.[8]

[1] *Ibid.* XIII (1), no. 1376.
[2] Possibly legal suits for not maintaining masses in the chapel.
[3] *Ibid.* XIII (2) no. 86.
[4] C. Wriothesley, *A Chronicle of England* (Camden Soc. 1875), I, 82.
[5] *Ibid.*
[6] *L. and P.* XIII (1), 1177.   [7] Wriothesley, *op. cit.* I, 82.
[8] *Ibid.* But E. Hall, *Chronicle* (1809), 826, says that this took place in September. On 17 September 1538, Partridge wrote to Bullinger: 'You have heard no doubt of the Lady of Walsingham and the breaking in pieces of the Holy idols.' In January 1540 Cromwell was informed from Walsingham, 'The said image is not well out of some of their heads', an old woman having got into trouble because of this (*L. and P.* XV, no. 86).

THE LAST DAYS

By this time Prior Vowell's pathetic hopes that his house would avoid destruction had been blasted. On 25 July, Sir Richard Gresham wrote to Cromwell acknowledging instructions 'that the king's pleasure is that the priory of Walsingham shall be dissolved' and informed him that he had notified the prior of this.[1] On 4 August 1538 the end came. In the priory chapterhouse before the royal commissioner, Sir William Petre, the prior and his canons signed the deed surrendering their house with all its possessions to the king.[2]

On 12 August Richard Vowell, writing as 'Prest', asked Cromwell for various favours including the parsonage of Walsingham[3] and also begged expeditious action to solve the financial needs of his brethren and himself. Four days later Gresham wrote to Cromwell that the prior of Walsingham was 'both impotent and lame' and urged that he be given the parsonage, declaring him to be 'very discreet, learned, of good name and can set forth the Word of God very well, whereof the town has great need'.[4] In the event he became vicar of South Creake and a good number of his brethren are known to have received pensions or benefices or both.[5] On 7 November 1539, Thomas Sydney of Little Walsingham and his wife bought the building and site of the

---

[1] *L. and P.* XIII (1), no. 1453.

[2] *Ibid.* XIII (2), 31. The text of the Close Roll copy is printed in *Arch. Journ.* XIII (1856), 129–31. The original deed has evidently not survived and this copy unfortunately does not give the signatures of the brethren, so we cannot be certain how many they were at this stage.

[3] *L. and P.* XIII (2), 86. This seems to have included all three churches.

[4] *Ibid.* 114.

[5] G. Baskerville, 'Married clergy and pensioned religious in Norwich diocese 1555' in *Eng. Hist. Rev.* XLVIII (1933), 43–64, 199–228. Blomefield noted (*Hist. of Norfolk*, IX, 278) that in 1555 eleven ex-canons of Walsingham were receiving pensions. I have found nothing to justify Waterton's remark (*op. cit.* 217) that 'at the suppression fifteen of the canons of Walsingham were condemned for high treason of whom five were executed'.

late priory of Walsingham with two closes of land formerly belonging to it for £90.[1] Spelman tells us that when he was at school at Walsingham it was said that Sydney 'was by the townsmen employed to have bought the site of the abbey to the use of the town, but obtained and kept it to himself'.[2]

Thus fell one of the most magnificent monasteries of medieval England. But its memory was long a-dying; and about the end of the century an anonymous poem, perhaps by Philip earl of Arundel, poured out the bitterness which the deed had brought to those to whom the cult of Our Lady stood as an ennobling force in a crude society.

In the wrackes[3] of Walsingam, whom should I chuse
But the Queene of Walsingam to be guide to my muse.
Then thou Prince of Walsingam grant me to frame
Bitter plaintes to rewe thy wronge, bitter wo for thy name.
Bitter was it oh to see the seely[4] sheepe
Murdered by the raveninge wolves, while the sheephards did sleep.
Bitter was it oh to vewe the sacred vyne,
While the gardiners plaied all close, rooted up by the swine.
Bitter, bitter oh to behould the grasse to growe,
Where the walls of Walsingam so stately did shew.
Such were the works of Walsingam while shee did stand,
Such are the wrackes as now do shewe of that holy land.
Levell levell with the ground the towres doe lye,
Which with their golden, glitteringe tops pearsed once to the skye.
Where weare gates, no gates are nowe; the waies unknowen,
Where the press of peares[5] did passe while her fame far was blowen.

---

[1] *L. and P.* XIV (2), 619 (15). Cf. *C.P.R.* (*1550–3*), 416–17. Much of the priory property went to Sir Thomas Gresham (*ibid.* 240).
[2] H. Spelman, *History of Sacrilege* (ed. C. F. S. Warren, 1895), 146.
[3] Devastation.   [4] Innocent.   [5] Nobles.

THE LAST DAYS

Oules do scrike where the sweetest himnes lately weer songe,
Toades and serpents hold their dennes wher the palmers did thronge.
Weepe, weepe O Walsingam, whose dayes are nightes,
Blessinge turned to blasphemies, holy deeds to dispites.[1]
Sinne is wher our Ladie sate, heaven turned is to hell,
Sathan sittes wher our Lord did swaye, Walsingam oh farewell.[2]

On 6 July 1922 a replica of the ancient image of Our Lady was ceremonially installed in the Anglican parish church, and soon after organized pilgrimages began there. In 1931 the statue was moved to a permanent shrine built in the village. The chapel was later extended and various auxiliary buildings added; it is now visited by some thousands of pilgrims annually. The Roman Catholic focus of devotion is the medieval Slipper Chapel at Houghton (on which see Appendix IV) which was reopened in 1934 and is now the centre of very large pilgrimages.

[1] Outrages.
[2] Bodl. Lib. Oxf., MS. Rawl. poet. 219 fo. 16^{r-v}. See Percy's *Ballads and Romances* (ed. Hales and Furnivall, 1868), III, 465–72 for ballads concerning Walsingham, and for other literary references E. H. Sugden, *A Topographical Dictionary to the works of Shakespeare...* (Manchester, 1925), 555. A. Gasquet, *Henry VIII and the English Monasteries* (London, 1888), II, 432, refers to 'windows, doors, stone called freestone, glass, iron and tiles' from Walsingham being disposed of in lots at the Dissolution; I have been unable to check this, as his reference (P.R.O. Mins. Accts. 31–2 Hen. VIII, 255 m.10d) is incorrect.

PART II

ARCHAEOLOGICAL

CHAPTER IV

THE CHURCH AND CLOISTERS

THE architectural history of the priory of Walsingham cannot as yet be written with anything like the detail desirable, partly because very little documentary evidence concerning it has so far been discovered, but principally because the site has not been scientifically excavated. If the poem quoted above can be believed, the priory was quickly destroyed, and certainly no drawing or print has survived to show substantially more of the remains than are visible today. The earliest representations of the ruins that the writer has been able to discover are the engraving by Van der Gucht after Bardslade (1720) and the well-known East View by Buck (1738),[1] the former giving no useful information not found in Buck. From these it seems that the church was much in its present condition at that date[2] and, as far as can be seen, not much more remained of the monastic buildings, though a useful sketch of later date shows a few remains of the south end of the western range, and gives a little extra information about the refectory.[3] Much of the present house was built somewhere in the very late eighteenth or early nineteenth century, for a writer in 1814 notes that the then owner 'Henry Lee Warner Esq. has built a mansion here, on

[1] Plate 1.
[2] Buck shows some remains at the south-east angle of the cloister not now visible. They are probably not very accurately depicted, though the remains of the eastern range north of the passage may well have been more considerable then than now.
[3] Below, 89.

the site of the priory',[1] but it evidently incorporates a good deal of earlier work. A reference, evidently of 1790, to 'the avenues of trees and shrubs' suggests that the layout of the site was then what it had been in Buck's day.[2] But in 1814 Britton thought fit to dedicate his plate of the eastern gable of the priory to 'John Haverfield Esq., who has displayed much taste in laying out the grounds around these ruins',[3] and it is probable that not a little levelling of the site occurred at this time which involved at least the demolition of the scanty remains of the western range.[4]

In 1853–4 a series of excavations was carried out. They appear to have involved clearing the extreme western end of the church and of the area around the eastern part of its north wall, and the running of two understandably unhelpful trenches north from the church. The first report of these was given by the Rev. J. Lee Warner in the *Archaeological Journal* for 1856[5] which was supplemented by Henry Harrod in his *Gleanings among the Castles and Convents of Norfolk*,[6] both of which have plans worthy of study. A large but very rough plan of the same excavations is preserved at the Abbey House. Harrod refers to a plan of excavations made 'nearly a quarter of a century ago...by a person in the employment of Mr Lee Warner, of the name of Grannan',[7] but I have been unable to get any further information about this.

The cartulary gives no useful indications about the original buildings, though, as we have seen, it records the purchase of certain property in the town to permit

[1] J. Britton, *The Architectural Antiquities of Great Britain* (1814), IV, 104.
[2] G. J. Parkyns, *Monastic and Baronial Remains* (2 vols. 1816), I, 2.
[3] *Op. cit.* IV, 103.   [4] Below, 89.
[5] XIII (1856), 115–34.   [6] (Norwich, 1857), 154–97.
[7] *Op. cit.* 170.

an enlargement of the priory precinct. Only the slightest clues can be found elsewhere. A late twelfth-century seal of the priory has survived in the British Museum[1] and bears on one side a simple representation of a cruciform church with a central tower and round-headed arches and windows. This is the sort of building that one would have expected to have existed at Walsingham at the time, but it would be unwise to assume that the seal gives more than a rough representation of the church. The only stone recognizable as of this date so far discovered on the site is a loose compound waterleaf capital which belongs to the late twelfth century.[2] At the time of writing it is in the small garden by the pond, but nothing is known of its original position. The next oldest relic is the round-headed doorway in the garden east of the church. This is of two orders though the detached shafts have gone.[3] The rather sophisticated mouldings, which include dog-tooth ornament, suggest that it belongs to the early years of the thirteenth century; it should be noted that this archway is not in its original position.[4]

The first clear reference to the architectural history of the priory occurs in 1232, when the Close Rolls for the year record that the king had ordered the sheriff to supply the prior of Walsingham with forty oak trees to make beams (*cheverones*) for the work on his church.[5] Two years later the king had sent the house ten oaks from his forest in Colchester and another ten from Newcastle upon Tyne 'to make a certain building (*camera*) as the gift of the king'.[6] In our present state of knowledge it is not possible to assess the significance of these

[1] Below, 108.
[2] Plate 7(*a*).
[3] Plate 3(*b*).
[4] Below, 94–5.
[5] *C.C.R.* (*1231–4*), 82.
[6] *Ibid.* 379.

THE CHURCH AND CLOISTERS

two entries. The first certainly suggests building or repair operations, but their precise nature is not clear. As the present buildings at Cartmel, Lanercost, Hexham and Brinkburn show us, it was by no means unusual for the lesser houses of Austin canons to require fifty years or more to erect their permanent churches. In view of the smallness of Walsingham in its early years it is not impossible that the priory did not acquire all its subsidiary buildings until a good half century or more after its foundation. If we place our faith in the seal we must conclude that the 1232 grant refers to some minor work. What the building was to which the 1234 entry refers can only be guessed at. It may well have belonged to the outer court and does not sound as if it was a place of importance.

It is a little surprising that the Chancery enrolments for the late thirteenth century have so far yielded no clear information regarding building at the priory at this time; there is no doubt that this took place, for the present remains of the western tower and the refectory can be roughly assigned to the later years of Edward I (1272–1307).[1] It is possible that the adjoining cloister (now vanished) had been constructed a little earlier, as there are in the stables two twin caps of what was almost certainly the cloister arcade, and which belong to about the middle years of the century. It is worth noting that the plan of the priory, as shown in the air photograph, suggests an extensive rebuilding of the cloister that probably dates from the late thirteenth century, and it may explain why the priory was seriously in debt in 1280.[2] It was the all but invariable medieval practice for the east range of the cloister to be aligned on the central tower, where this existed. At Walsingham,

[1] Below, 89.   [2] Above, 23.

MEDIEVAL REBUILDING

however, we find the range lying half a bay to the east of this.[1] It is difficult to avoid the conjecture that the priory had a small eastern range in the normal position but, desiring to increase the size of the cloister and its buildings, the canons built an entirely new set of buildings immediately to the east of the old ones. It is not clear why this course was followed, instead of the more usual one of extending the cloister on its western side. That this change took place originally in the late thirteenth century is suggested principally by the refectory, which is of this period and was clearly designed to fit the south side of the enlarged cloister. In the writer's opinion it is likely that the first priory church and cloister were finished by the early years of the thirteenth century and that the former was of the simple cruciform type portrayed on the seal. In the middle and later decades of the same century, following the rapid growth in Walsingham's fame under Henry III, the size of the convent increased and an enlarged cloister was begun, evidently working eastward, contrary to usual practice. As we shall see, the capitals from the north-west corner of the cloister belong to the middle of the century, the western tower and refectory to a generation or so later, and the south end of the eastern range to the early fourteenth century.

However this may be, there is no doubt about the date of the next building phase, probably the most splendid in the history of the priory, involving the extensive rebuilding of the church. The list of canons already mentioned opens with the note: 'Be it remembered that in the year of [our] Lord one thousand three hundred and eighty-four John Snoryng was the 13th

[1] See Plate 3 (a). Projection of a lantern slide of this leaves little doubt about this unusual arrangement.

THE CHURCH AND CLOISTERS

prior of Walsygham [*sic*], John Ieryngham alias Waryn was subprior and the principal assistant over the building of our church.'[1] Now the famous eastern gable of the church could be assigned to about the priorate of Snoring (1374–c. 1401) on archaeological grounds alone, though it was evidently begun a little earlier; for in 1360 Lady Clare left bequests 'a l'overaigne de l'église de Walsingham',[2] and Sir Thomas Uvedale in his will of 1367 left 10 marks for work on the choir of Walsingham.[3] The list also shows that work on the furnishing of the church was going on at this time. It is noted of the canon Thomas Lynne that 'with his own hands he assisted the craftsmen of the high altar',[4] whilst one John Yarmouth, subprior (presumably the canon of that name mentioned in 1383),[5] had the roof of the body of the church painted and the chapel of St Nicholas with the image ('tabula') therein.[6] This evidence, adequate in itself, is supported by a reference in 1385 to 'the chapel of St Anne newly built by the said prior and convent within the said monastery'.[7] Of the chancel built at this time the principal relic is the eastern gable as already noted; a large gargoyle, shaped like a lion's head[8] and now in the small garden near the wells, from its size and style may well have belonged to this date and place. The only other building reference in the list concerns the making of a library by William Lynne who evidently flourished in the time of Prior Hunt (1437–74).[9] A few other isolated references of interest in this connexion have survived. In 1437 we have

---

[1] Below, 136. [2] Above, 36.
[3] *Surrey Arch. Coll.* III, 151, 'lego decem marcas fabricae chori ecclesiae de Walsingham'.
[4] Below, 136. [5] Above, 29.
[6] Below, 136. [7] *C.P.R.* (*1381–5*), 557–8.
[8] Plate 7(*c*). [9] Below, 137.

mention of 'the chapel of St Thomas within the precincts of the priory of Walsingham'.[1] Half a century later—in 1493—Bishop Alcock of Ely granted an indulgence to all who hear mass at the Cheyney altar in Walsingham Priory for the souls of Sir John Cheyney, Lady Agnes his wife and certain others.[2] The episcopal visitation of 1514 refers to 'the building commonly called *the halibred house*',[3] and we also hear of a treasury here[4]—an obvious necessity with so many valuables about. It is to be hoped that future research will greatly augment the above, very scrappy, documentary evidence on the history of the building of the priory.

Two valuable supplementary sources for a knowledge of the final plan of the church and cloisters should be mentioned. An air photograph has shown very clearly much of the foundations of the church and cloister [5] and provides a useful supplement to the measurements of the church recorded by William of Worcester. William toured Norfolk in 1479 [6] and the considerable accuracy of his notes on the Franciscan friary at Walsingham was shown when that site was excavated.[7] His notes on the priory of Our Lady are as follows:

The length of the new building of Walsyngham consists of 16 yards, its width below the platform of 10 yards. The length of the chapel of blessed Mary consists of 7 yards 30 inches, its width of 4 yards 10 inches. The length of the whole church of Walsingham as far as the beginning of the chancel consists of 136 paces, its breadth of 36 paces. The length of the nave from the west door as far as the belfry in the middle of the church consists of 70 paces. The crossing or belfry

---

[1] Norwich Epis. Reg. xv, fo. 11ʳ, 'capella sancti Thome infra precinctum prioratus de Walsyngham'.
[2] Ely, Epis. Reg. Alcock, fo. 93.   [3] *Norwich Visitations*, 117.
[4] *Ibid.* 147.   [5] Plate 3(*a*).
[6] *Itineraria... Willelmi de Worcestre* (ed. J. Nasmith, 1778), 303 ff., 312.
[7] A. R. Martin, *Franciscan Architecture in England* (1937), 130.

THE CHURCH AND CLOISTERS

area consists of 16 paces each way. The width of the nave of the church alone without the two aisles is 16 paces. The length of the cloister, which is completely square, 54 paces. The length of the *Chapiterhouse* alone consists of 20 paces and its breadth 10 paces, but the length of the portico of the *Chapiterhouse* from the cloister consists of 10 paces, thus totalling 30 paces.[1]

The combination of these two sources with the evidence of excavations and visible remains makes it possible to construct a reasonably accurate general plan of the church and adjacent buildings.[2]

The GATEHOUSE remains, though it has lost its original roof and parapet. It is considerably smaller than that of many monasteries of similar size, comparing unfavourably in this respect, for example, with the gatehouse of such less wealthy, East Anglian Austin priories as Pentney, Butley and St Osyth. This is almost certainly due to the fact that Walsingham Priory did not, as was usual, own the local court, and therefore had no need for the large room over the gateway which

[1] *Itin. Willelmi de Worc.* 335-6:
WALSYNGHAM. longitudo noui operis de Walsyngham continet 16 virgas.
latitudo continet infra aream. 10 virgas.
longitudo capelle beate marie continet 7 virgas 30 pollices.
latitudo continet 4 virgas 10 pollices.
longitudo tocius Ecclesie de Walsyngham usque ad principium cancelle continet 136 gressus.
latitudo eius continet 36 gressus.
longitudo navis ab occidentali porta usque ad campanile in medio Ecclesie continet 70 gressus.
Intersticium siue spacium campanilis continet 16 gressus quadrate.
latitudo proprie nauis Ecclesie preter 2 elas continet 16 gressus.
longitudo Claustri ex omni parte quadrate continet 54 gressus.
longitudo propria de le Chapiterhous continet 20 gressus, latitudo eius continet 10 gressus sed longitudo introitus de le chapiter hous a claustro continet 10 gressus; sic in toto continet 30 gressus.

[2] See Plan, facing p. 106.

THE GATEHOUSE AND PORTER'S LODGE

normally served as a court house. The date of the present building is not certain, but architectural evidence suggests it was built about the first half of the fifteenth century. The porter's lodge adjoins it on the north side.

Entrance is through a single archway, which, by an unusual arrangement, has the door set across the middle, with a shallow, single bay sloping outward on either side of it; both bays have lost their original vault but retained the springers. In the north wall of the outer bay is a small window, whilst on the same wall of the inner bay are the remains of a small doorway with shouldered head, now blocked up. Both arches of the gateway have wave mouldings with a sunk chamfer and three-quarter hollows and have four-pointed heads. Above the outer one are three plain shields set in square panels and surmounted by a dripstone, on either side of which are two large canopied niches, devoid of statues. Two grotesque human figures project from north-east and north-west corners of the wall and another from a quatrefoil below the middle of the parapet. Between the latter and the row of shields are curious perforated stone panels. The room over the archway is very plain and has a modern roof. Its west wall has a flue with a much altered fireplace. At its northern end and in a corresponding position in the opposite wall are squints terminating in quatrefoils, giving views down either end of High Street. The eastern wall of the gatehouse has in its centre a large square window with a transom and mullion; its soffit is scalloped and has over it some four-petal ornament. Outside on either side of this window are two canopied niches similar to those already mentioned; beneath is a large, plain, stone shield. The workmanship is notably inferior to that of the remains of the church and cloister.

THE CHURCH AND CLOISTERS

The PORTER'S LODGE adjoins the gatehouse on the north side. It is approached from the precinct by a small doorway in a wall, which, like its entrance doorway, has a four-centred arch; the latter has an elaborate dripmoulding. Inside, a vice leads up to the first floor on the left and to the living-room on the right. The original windows of the ground floor of the lodge have gone, but its first floor retains two windows, of one and of three trefoil-headed lights respectively, both with moulded dripstones. The present roof is modern.

From the gatehouse the ground slopes steadily down to the site of the church. There is no doubt that horticultural operations at various dates have greatly interfered with original levels here. Buck's print of the abbey[1] shows that by his day (1738) formal gardens had been laid out, with hedges circling the gable end of the church. The accounts by Harrod and Lee Warner make it clear that gardening operations obstructed their research in 1853–4 whilst as late as 1879 it was noted that 'the site of the renowned sanctuary of Our Ladye has recently been deeply buried beneath a terraced parterre'.[2]

The plan given by Lee Warner[3] shows foundations running from the south end of the western wall of the church towards the gatehouse. This is just possibly part of a porch but is more likely to have been part of a wall separating the buildings from land on the south of the church (which were given over to the convent) from that to the north which was open to the public. The visitor would enter by the great gate, proceed to the church, and thence to the Lady chapel on the north side of the nave and the chapel of St Laurence to the east.

[1] Plate 1.   [2] Waterton, *op. cit.* 220.
[3] *Op. cit.* 115.

THE PRIORY CHURCH

Little remains of the CHURCH above ground but it is possible to get a good idea of its plan.[1] The combination of available sources shows a rectangular church some 250 feet long by 70 feet broad with a short unaisled east end. This is by no means the normal plan for a house of Austin canons and excavation of this part of the site is highly desirable. From the scanty evidence at present available it would appear that the rebuilt church had transepts flush with the aisles and not projecting beyond them. This is a highly unusual feature, though a similar arrangement is found at Glasgow Cathedral *c.* 1260, and Holy Trinity, Hull, half a century later, has transepts which project only very slightly.[2] There is a superficial resemblance between the plan of Walsingham and that of the great friars' churches of the period but this cannot be pushed too far, as the replacement of a crossing in the latter by a narrow passage with a small belfry overhead inevitably leads to a tendency to abandon the transept.

In this connexion we should remind ourselves that Walsingham, though a great pilgrimage centre, was maintained by a comparatively small convent[3] which would not need the additional altar space provided by transepts in an enlarged church. The large nave would accommodate the flood of pilgrims and would contain ample space for the various private altars likely to be endowed at a place of this sort.

As we have seen, it is at least likely that a small transeptal church was originally built here; but only excavation can solve this question. The foundations of a

[1] See Plan, facing p. 106.

[2] I am indebted to Mr John Harvey for drawing my attention to these parallels.

[3] The brethren of Walsingham numbered between twenty and thirty as compared with about seventy at the shrine of St Thomas of Canterbury.

THE CHURCH AND CLOISTERS

central tower show very clearly on the air photograph and their existence is confirmed by William of Worcester's reference to 'the belfry in the middle of the church'. Remains of another belfry tower at the west end can still be seen. Twin axial towers of this type, though rare, are not unknown in medieval England, and this particular instance finds very close parallels in the neighbouring Benedictine abbeys of Bury St Edmunds and Ely with later ones at Wymondham and St Benet's, Hulme. There were, apparently, four bays east of the central tower and five west of it, including the one occupied by the western tower. The normal screen would divide the conventual choir from the nave and one may suspect that this occupied the western piers of the central tower, as anything further east would have exposed the main entrance to the cloister to public view. It should be remembered that Walsingham, unlike many houses of Austin canons, was not parochial, and that therefore the altar before the screen was not strictly a parish altar. As we shall see, the relic of the 'Holy Milk of Blessed Mary' was preserved at the high altar.[1] Such a position was clearly a convenient one, being on the pilgrims' way from the main western entrance of the church to the chapel of St Laurence, which lay to the east.[2]

The only remains of the church above ground are the extreme eastern end of the chancel and the bases of the western tower. The former has lost the tracery of its once magnificent east window but its frame and the gable remain, the latter having a curious, small, circular window with its tracery in its head. In either angle is a stone vice opening into the church. Each corner is supported by a pair of buttresses set at right angles to the wall. These are of three stages, the outer face having

[1] Below, 91. [2] See Plan, facing p. 106.

THE EAST END OF THE CHURCH

large niches with heavily cusped ogee heads surmounted by crocketed gables; the niches have bases for statues, though it is uncertain whether these were ever added. The outer wall space between these faces is panelled with the fine local flint work; the lower stage has blind arches of two lights with a quatrefoil in each triangular canopied head; the canopies have crockets and finials. The two upper stages are panelled into lights with cusped heads of a rather later style. In the more westerly of the northern buttresses is a small aumbry, similar to one in the parish church, evidently reset, as it is now in what was an external face.

In the excavations a century ago much of the eastern part of the north wall of the church was uncovered, and there were found on the north side of the second bay, west of the north aisle, remains of what is described as 'a porch or vestibule, in one corner of which there still exists *in situ* a red and yellow glazed tile, a portion of its chequered pavement';[1] the foundations of this projection show up clearly in the air photograph. We are also told that the wall of the church at this point was 'formed below the ground line with a massive arch, turned to a span of 6 feet, apparently the entrance to a vault or crypt beneath the original pavement of the church. It is filled with loose mould and circumstances did not permit an exploration of its interior.'[2] If this projection was a porch, which is likely enough, it was probably built primarily to provide access from the church to the chapel of St Laurence and to the wells which lay east of the church and perhaps to the cemetery (which may have been on the north-east). This necessitated the convent opening the north side of the chancel to the public; but this would not be much of an

[1] *Arch. Journ.* XIII, 122.   [2] *Ibid.*

added inconvenience since one of the relics venerated by the public was kept at the high altar.

Of the main body of the church nothing remains above ground. The west end had got badly overgrown by the time of the 1853 excavations and the present artificial banking-up of the level beyond the west wall of the church and the presence of a good many trees would make the examination of this area one of considerable difficulty. The work done a hundred years ago did, however, reveal 'portions of the two western piers with the corresponding abutments of the western wall, the jambs of the western doorway and the exterior buttress'.[1] The chief remains are ruins of the two southern piers which stand to the height of about 5 feet; their massiveness makes it clear that they were intended to support a western tower. They are of comparatively simple design with engaged columns separated by hollow chamfers; parts of them appear to have been slightly reset. Of the northern piers less remains and considerable signs of rebuilding are apparent. Between the piers and the nave wall were discovered foundations of some inferior walling, as also along the inside of the last bay of the south aisle; this is of uncertain, possibly post-Reformation, date. The 'jambs of the western doorway' are not now visible and the same applies to the signs of a small doorway in the south wall of the westernmost bay of the south aisle found in 1853–4.[2]

It is clear that there was some medieval rebuilding at the western part of the church. Harrod informs us that the floor shown in the view 'is of the Perpendicular period and six inches above the original one, and deprives

[1] *Arch. Journ.* XIII, 118, where a woodcut of these is given; since then the west wall has become much overgrown. [2] *Ibid.* 119.

THE EAST RANGE OF THE CLOISTER

the base of much of its beauty of proportion',[1] and the rough plan of the excavations preserved at the Abbey House shows that at least the first pillar east of the south-eastern pier of the tower was rebuilt on an older circular base. Pending excavation, we must remain uncertain whether the whole of the church was rebuilt as part of Prior Snoring's plan (as seems likely), and also about the history of the central tower. As we shall see, the chapel of Our Lady lay on the north side of the church and was enclosed in a larger building.[2]

On the south side of the church lay the cloister and its attendant buildings, of which the only portions now above ground are the refectory and the south end of the east range (now built into the modern house). The layout of the whole court can be approximately ascertained with the aid of the air photograph, William of Worcester's measurements and the rough plan preserved at the Abbey House. At the north-east angle of the EASTERN RANGE was a small, almost square building. It is not impossible that this was the sacristy, as apparently its door gave into the church. It is conceivable that over or near it was the library known to have been built by Brother William Lynn.[3] The books needed in the cloister were normally kept in a special cupboard in this angle of the cloister and were read in the northern alley. Immediately to the south was the vestibule to the chapter-house; the latter lay east of the cloister range and the air photograph confirms William of Worcester's observation that it was twice as long as it was broad, with a long vestibule. Further south, the

[1] Harrod, *Gleanings among the Castles and Convents of Norfolk*, 172.
[2] Below, 95 ff.
[3] Above, 76.

range continued as an undercroft of three bays separated from a passage by a thin wall.

Only the southern end of the outer walls of the range remains, but the eastern side of this contains two interesting squints. Their purpose can only be guessed at, but it may not be coincidence that the northern one points directly at the site of the wells and the now vanished chapel of St Laurence. It is exactly similar in measurements to one further south in the same wall.[1] South of the first squint was a partition wall (not shown in Harrod's plan) in the thickness of which was perhaps a door leading to a passage which crossed the eastern range at this point. At either end of the passage arches remain but they have been very extensively modernized and repaired. The eastern one has a semicircular outer face but this is almost certainly modern; its inner face has remains of one order of a pointed arch, which is moulded and may well be fourteenth-century. The western arch has its jambs and eastern face heavily repaired with modern brick but retains considerable remains of a pointed arch of two orders; this is noteworthy as being of medieval brick and has a dripmoulding formed of tiles. The mouldings are principally hollow chamfers and the arch had apparently no capitals; its date is uncertain.

South of the passage and now incorporated in the Abbey House is a fine UNDERCROFT[2] having two aisles of three bays. Its vault is a quadripartite one with plain chamfered ribs and small, unpretentious bosses of early fourteenth-century character. The central pillars are octagonal. The walls have been much altered and patched. At the southern end of the aisles were two windows now also much altered: that to the east retains

[1] Below, 87.   [2] Plate 5.

some of its original tracery but has been converted into a door; the western one retains its original sill but has been blocked up and modernized as has a similar window at the southern end of the east wall. In the southeast corner is a small door which probably originally led to a stair to the floor above. Near the southern window of the east wall is a small squint. It is of exactly the same size as the one in the continuation of this wall north of the passage, but points in the opposite direction and has been blocked on the outside; the rebate for a shutter and traces of hinges and a lock remain—its purpose is problematic. At the north end of this east wall is a small pointed doorway with a semicircular niche on either side of its inner face, probably intended to hold lights.[1] The windows in the north wall are modern. The west wall of the undercroft seems to have been much patched, and has a doorway in the middle of it. This has a head of brick that may be medieval, but the jambs have been heavily modernized and are of uncertain date. The doorway leads to a vaulted passage of two narrow bays. This has remains of a doorway at its southern end, now blocked, which seems to have led into an outer court; the north wall of the passage is modern, so one cannot be certain if there was originally another doorway here, but this is likely enough; a passage at this point would be very convenient and it is worth noting that this small vaulted chamber is known as the *slype*, the medieval word for a passage of this kind. There is no documentary evidence of the date of this eastern range but all the architectural details are consistent with one of about 1320–30, and it may very well form a late part of a scheme for the general rebuilding of the cloister begun in the thirteenth century.

[1] Plate 5.

The purpose of the undercroft south of the passage and its lost first floor cannot be certainly established, but it is not unlikely that it was used as the prior's apartments, the ground floor providing the living-room with the stair leading to the bedroom and chapel above. It would not be surprising to find this set of rooms in the opposite (that is, western) range of the cloister, as, for example, at Bridlington and Micheham. But at Walsingham the constant influx of pilgrims into the church would doubtless make such a site noisy and inconvenient.

East of the entrance door to the undercroft are some foundations of a wall running east. South of these, to judge by the Abbey House plan, was a small rectangular building attached to the undercroft, and perhaps forming another side of a small court. The only important relic of it visible is a fine doorway with a four-centred head and shallow mouldings of fifteenth-century type, built into an inner wall of the Abbey House, but probably *in situ*.

Adjoining the undercroft on its western side is the monastic REFECTORY,[1] most of which remains, though much of its north wall has gone and the eastern one has been refaced in modern times. This was the normal position for such a building and its purpose is made quite certain by the survival of the washing-place adjoining its main entrance (at the west end of the north wall) and the very fine refectory pulpit at the opposite end of the south wall. The latter is of three bays with boldly cusped heads and graceful, slender pillars and is little damaged. Near by, among some pseudo-Gothic work are remains of a large fifteenth-century inscription; it is in a fragmentary condition and commemorates a benefactor named

[1] Plate 4 (*a*).

THE REFECTORY AND WESTERN RANGE

Robert, and his wife and children. There can be little doubt that the building belongs to about 1280–90 when, as we have seen, the priory was high in favour with Edward I. The south wall has two small windows, both of two lights, one having simple bar tracery, the other a large trefoil in its head. There are two doorways. One is a small plain one in the south wall which probably led to a kitchen yard. West of it are what have been taken to be remains of a hatch through which food was passed from the adjoining kitchen. The other doorway is at the west end of the north wall and is an elaborate piece of work with a series of alternate pointed and filleted rolls separated by deep hollows and having a scroll-moulded label. East of it are the damaged remains of the arcaded washing-place or *lavatorium*. The west wall contains a fine, late thirteenth-century window, somewhat restored. Its head has one large and two small quatrefoils, beneath which are four pointed lights with uncusped heads and trefoils above. A useful sketch of the south-west angle of the cloister made in 1790[1] shows that the refectory had then a somewhat damaged roof and that the remains of the washing-place were covered by a lean-to shed.

This drawing also depicts some slight remains of the undercroft of the WESTERN RANGE, showing ruins of a vault and a small nondescript doorway in the eastern wall; but these details are inadequate for dating purposes. The drawing was perhaps made before the present house was built. The erection of the latter was accompanied by more of that horticulture to the detriment of archaeology which is so melancholy a feature of Walsingham's history, and it is probable that these

---

[1] Parkyns, *loc. cit.*; cf. Blomefield, *op. cit.* IX, 278, who (1808) describes the building as 'very entire with an old very good roof on it'.

THE CHURCH AND CLOISTERS

remains of the western range disappeared then. Little further is known of the western range of the cloister. Harrod's plan shows it as a simple rectangular building communicating with the church by a doorway in its northern wall, which lay several inches south of the church wall and was not, as one would have expected, identical with it at this point. He assigns it to the Decorated period and terms it a guest hall. His reasons for so doing are not convincing, but what may well have been a guest-house at the nearby Franciscan friary was a prominent and unusual feature of its plan.[1] The priory at Walsingham almost certainly had an unusually large amount of guest accommodation within the precinct, so there may have been additional space allotted for the purpose here, but this is doubtful.

Of the CLOISTER itself little is known. The plan in the Abbey House indicates its arcades by a number of blobs, but how accurate these are is not clear. In Harrod's plan, two of the buttresses projecting into the close are shown with the foundation of the western and part of the northern cloister arcades. It is likely that this work belonged, in part at least, to the mid thirteenth century. There are at present preserved in the stables of the Abbey House two small twin capitals.[2] These are probably several decades earlier than the refectory. They may well be 'the bases and shafts of an external arcade on the south side of the west end...particularly early English in character' found by Harrod.[3] We have seen that the cloister was evidently extended eastward in the late thirteenth century, but these capitals probably came from the part of it which may not have been rebuilt.

---

[1] A. R. Martin, *op. cit.* 135.   [2] Plate 7 (*b*).
[3] *Op. cit.* 158.

CHAPTER V

THE PLACES OF PILGRIMAGE

EXAMINATION shows that the priory of Walsingham was laid out on a very careful plan which allowed the movement of the great crowds of pilgrims with a minimum of inconvenience to the regular canons. The latter, as we have seen, had their buildings in the normal position south of the church. The sites which the former frequented lay to the north and east. The Valor Ecclesiasticus shows that offerings were made in three places.[1]

The earliest reference to the relic of the 'Milk of the Blessed Mary' so far found is in the account roll of 28 Edward I which shows that it was then at the high altar.[2] And Erasmus tells us that, in his day, the relic was kept on 'the high altar in the centre of which is Christ' (that is, the Blessed Sacrament).[3] The altar referred to is thus the high altar of the convent, east of the screen. Erasmus also tells us that the history of this relic was recorded on a tablet 'high up' nearby, together with details of the episcopal indulgences granted in connexion with it.[4] Those apt to overrate the superstition of medieval man should note that offerings here in 1535 were a mere 42s. 3d. out of a combined total of over £260.[5]

The next smallest offerings were those totalling £8. 9s. 1d. in the chapel of St Laurence.[6] The Pynson ballad enables us to locate this chapel by referring to it as being on the original site of the chapel of Our Lady,

---

[1] Above, 60. [2] Above, 40. [3] Nichols, 20.
[4] *Idem*, 27; above, 56. [5] Above, 60. [6] *Ibid.*

THE PLACES OF PILGRIMAGE

near two wells,[1] which last may safely be identified with the two still existing, east of the church. It should be noted, however, that little or nothing of this chapel remains above ground, the archway at present standing near the wells having been transferred from elsewhere as we shall see. This chapel is the one mentioned by Erasmus after his comments on the Knight's Door:

> To the east of it is a chapel full of wonders.... Presently the joint of a man's finger is exhibited to us, the largest of three. I kiss it, and then I ask 'Whose relics are these?' He [the guide] says, 'St Peter's.' 'The Apostle?' I ask. He said 'Yes.' Then observing the size of the joint which might have been that of a giant, I remarked, 'Peter must have been a man of very large size.'[2]

It is not unlikely that the relics here referred to were those which in the time of Edward I's visit in 1290 were on the altar of the Lady chapel.[3]

It would have been natural enough, when the chapel of Our Lady was getting filled with votive offerings, to move the relics to a new site. Of the wells themselves little more can be said. Erasmus says that they were 'full to the brink. They say the spring is sacred to the Holy Virgin. The water is wonderfully cold, and efficacious in curing pains of the head and stomach... they affirm that the spring burst suddenly from the earth at the command of the most Holy Virgin.'[4] As we have seen, we have a rather earlier reference than this to the well of Our Lady.[5] Erasmus is our only clear authority for regarding the wells as of any medical importance though it is likely enough that they were used for this purpose much earlier. He also tells us that they were covered by a shed of modern appearance.[6]

[1] Below, 127. [2] Nichols, 17. [3] Above, 39.
[4] Nichols, 18. [5] Above, 12. [6] Nichols, 18.

THE TANK AND ITS PURPOSE

No early reference has been discovered to the rectangular stone tank near the wells. It is mentioned in 1831 with the wells,[1] and in Blomefield,[2] while in 1816 we hear of 'two circular stone pits'.[3] But neither wells nor tank were likely to attract notice in extant medieval evidence.

Mr Arthur Bond of Walsingham informs me that, before the 1939–45 war, tests were made which showed that water flowed into the tank from the nearer well, and thence probably into the farther well. He also pointed out that when, in 1945, drought permitted an examination of the sides of the tank, it was very clear that these had been considerably heightened, the original lower portion being clearly distinguishable. Unfortunately this lower masonry has no datable feature. With such inconclusive evidence it would be unwise to hazard any precise guess as to the date of the tank, though it is not unlikely that the bottom part of it and the wells are of medieval origin.

As to its purpose, it should be noted that supplies of water from pilgrimage centres were greatly valued in the Middle Ages. At Compostella there was near the church 'a remarkable fountain the like of which is not to be found in the whole world'.[4] At Canterbury, in the twelfth century, it was noted that 'water sanctified by the blood of the holy martyr is carried forth, and, when given to the sick and poured into some that had been dead it has restored health to the former and life to many of the latter, through the merits of St Thomas'.[5]

---

[1] S. Lewis, *Topographical Dictionary of England* (1831), IV, 374.
[2] *Op. cit.* IX (1808), 278, 'a stone bath and two uncovered wells'.
[3] G. J. Parkyns, *Monastic and Baronial Remains*, I, 2.
[4] Codex of Calixtus II quoted in K. J. Conant, *Santiago of Compostella* (Harvard, 1926), 51.
[5] Gervase of Canterbury, *Opera Historica* (R.S. 73), I, 230.

A very elaborate flask in the York Museum is inscribed 'Optimus egrorum medicus fit Thoma bonorum'[1] (Thomas is the best healer of the holy sick), and the same inscription occurs on another flask of quite different design now in the London Museum.[2] The cult of Simon de Montfort was quickly associated with a well at the place where he fell, to which pilgrims resorted and from which water was transported.[3] It would, therefore, seem likely enough that the wells and tank at Walsingham provided water for a similar purpose, especially since Erasmus testifies that healing properties were ascribed to it and the Pynson ballad reports that 'many seke ben here cured by our ladyes myghte'.

The tank may have been constructed to form a convenient source of water for this, and have had its sides greatly heightened in post-Reformation times. We cannot entirely dismiss the possibility that the tank was used for washing by those who had come on pilgrimage barefoot. It is well placed for such a purpose and there is enough evidence to show that Henry VIII was not alone in arriving *nudis pedibus*.

The round arch near the tank was re-erected on its present site about the time the house was built. Harrod writing in 1857 refers to this arch as 'removed from the building south of the refectory not very many years ago',[4] and it must be the 'semicircular arch in a mass of masonry annexed to the wishing wells' mentioned by Britton in 1814.[5] The adjacent masonry may be original

---

[1] *Brit. Arch. Assn. Journ.* VI (o.s.), 125.
[2] A. 27323, illustrated in London Museum, *Medieval Catalogue*, pl. LXVIII.
[3] *Miracula Simonis de Montfort* (ed. J. O. Halliwell, Camden Soc. 1840), 68–9. [4] *Op. cit.* 158.
[5] J. Britton, *The Architectural Antiquities of Great Britain*, IV, 107; cf. Lewis, *Topograph. Dict. of England*, IV, 374.

THE CHAPEL OF OUR LADY

work with the present doorway replacing a ruined one, but this is another point which can only be cleared up by excavation of the site.

There can be no doubt that the chapel of Our Lady housed the statue which made Walsingham so famous, and the fact that the yearly offerings here in 1535 amounted to the enormous sum of £250. 10s. is sufficient indication of its importance. The history of this chapel is somewhat confused. The Pynson ballad in the late fifteenth century declares that it was intended to build the first chapel of Our Lady on the site which was finally occupied by the chapel of St Laurence,[1] but that, when it was under construction, its timbers were moved overnight by angelic hands to a place 'two hundred fote and more in dystaunce From the fyrste place'.[2] What lies behind this belief that the site of the Lady chapel was thus changed cannot be established. Certainly at the time of the Reformation the chapel of Our Lady was not by the wells. The question of its site at this time has been disputed but the answer can scarcely be in doubt.

In the first place we must certainly look for it within the priory precinct. This was the obvious rule in cases, as at Walsingham, where such a shrine was stocked with enormously valuable offerings of silver, gold and jewels. Indeed the petition against the foundation of the Franciscan house at Walsingham makes it quite clear that this was so here, noting that the priory gates had to be shut at night because of thieves who might threaten to steal treasures offered at the shrine.[3] A further obvious consideration was that the shrine should be in close proximity to the church and on the opposite side of it from the conventual buildings, that is, at Walsingham,

[1] Below, 127.   [2] *Ibid.*   [3] Above, 26.

on the north side of the church. This choice of site is confirmed by a cartulary reference to the 'grownd withowth the westgate of the yerd of owr ladys chapell wchych is now callyd the common place',[1] the 'common place' being the name of the open area north-west of the priory church, and Erasmus tells us the Lady chapel was on the right hand of the church looking west.[2] The Pynson ballad's phrase that the chapel was moved 'two hundred fote and more' from the wells is clearly not to be interpreted too strictly, but is a useful clue. It is also worth noting that, when Abbot Beere, rather later, built a chapel of Our Lady of Loretto at Glastonbury, it was similarly sited some half-way along the north side of the church.[3] This is precisely the situation which all the best evidence suggests for the final position of the Lady chapel at Walsingham. As there have been discovered in this place foundations which are wholly consistent with the theory, and where, in the usual monastic plan, nothing of this kind normally existed, it is all but certain that we have here the site where the statue of Our Lady was venerated by so many, especially since this part had the exceptional luxury of a pavement of Purbeck marble,[4] a thing only to be expected in a building of very great importance.

It is unfortunate that the present knowledge of this area is very unsatisfactory. It is clear that the excavators of 1853 were hampered by a garden path and tree roots, but even so, their account of this part of their work leaves much to be desired. Thus the original report refers to a 12-foot wall in this area,[5] but one of the excavators later wrote 'upon subsequent reflexion I believe that the

[1] Cartul. fo. 5ᵛ = *Mon.* 71. [2] Nichols, 13.
[3] Below, 106. [4] *Arch. Journ.* XIII, 124.
[5] *Ibid.* 123.

THE CHAPEL OF OUR LADY

great thickness of the east wall was apparent not real, and that it was in fact only a portion of wall lying flat, having been partially undermined and so fallen',[1] a remark which makes it difficult to place full faith in the very detailed plans of this building given by both Lee Warner and Harrod.

Indeed, the more their evidence on this point is examined the more perplexing does it look. Thus we are told that there was discovered 'a platform of solid grouted masonry which measures from east to west 20 feet and from north to south 40'.[2] But both plans show the enclosed area with its longer sides running east and west not north and south, and give its measurements as some 35 by 45 feet,[3] dimensions according well enough with William of Worcester's estimate of the measurements of the outer chapel (16 by 10 yards).[4] But it is useful to know that the chapel (whatever its dimensions) had a level about 2 feet above that of the church, that its pavement was of Purbeck marble bedded on solid mortar of 3 inches in thickness and that it was entered by a doorway of three steps pierced in the '12 foot wall [*sic*] which separated the church from it. This being the door of the entrance a corresponding door of egress was placed directly opposite, flanked by large buttresses; or possibly these foundations may have carried a shallow porch.... The west as well as the north appears to have had its doorway; and the north wall at its ground line was bedded in flat masonry at two separate levels as if it had been cased originally with squared blocks of stone of large dimensions.'[5] These

---

[1] Quoted by E. Waterton, *Pietas Mariana Britannica* (1879), 167.
[2] *Arch. Journ.* XIII, 123, quoted by Harrod, *op. cit.* 162.
[3] Harrod's plan is on a much larger scale and is to be preferred.
[4] Above, 77. [5] *Arch. Journ.* XIII, 124–5.

THE PLACES OF PILGRIMAGE

excavations suggested that the northern corners of the building had turrets. If so, one or both may have contained circular stairs to a room overhead. Such a chamber would have been admirably suited to be a treasury; a place known to have existed at Walsingham,[1] and a very necessary repository for the many cash offerings and for such other oblations as it was not desirable to exhibit.

But there is so little that can safely be said about the plan of the shrine, at least until further excavation has taken place, that much surmise is injudicious. It is worth noting that, though what was believed to be the original site of the Annunciation was pointed out to medieval pilgrims to Nazareth, so early an authority as Arculf (c. 670) evidently knew of no dwelling remaining there other than the cave.[2] By 1106–7, when the Russian abbot Daniel visited Nazareth, there were detailed legends current regarding rock chambers evidently under the church, which were held to have formed the house of Our Lady and St Joseph, before the entrance of which the Annunciation was held to have taken place.[3] But there was clearly nothing there to serve as a prototype for the house of Walsingham, which was therefore not in any strict sense a copy of an ancient one.

William of Worcester's measurements[4] show that the little chapel of Our Lady measured approximately 23 feet 6 inches by 12 feet 10 inches and was surrounded by a larger building which he terms 'the new work', of which he gives the measurements as 16 yards long and 10 yards broad 'infra aream'. The meaning of the last phrase has been debated. It is probably to be translated 'beneath the floor' and, in view of Erasmus's remark that

[1] Above, 77.
[2] *Pal. Pilg. Text Soc.* III, 45.
[3] *Ibid.* IV (2), 69–71.
[4] Above, 77–8.

THE CHAPEL OF OUR LADY

the chapel was 'constructed with a wooden platform' ('ligneo tabulatu constructum'), clearly implies some sort of superstructure. If, as is likely though unproven, the chapel was of wood,[1] it may well have been found desirable to put it on a raised wooden floor to prevent its timbers rotting; or it may be that there were some external wooden stairs to the first floor of the chapel. This problem cannot be certainly solved with the evidence so far discovered.

Mr John Harvey has pointed out to me that at Compostella in the nineteenth century, at feasts of special solemnity, visitors to the shrine went up by a staircase behind the altar and down by another on the other side,[2] whilst the relics at Lapworth church (Warwickshire) were in a small upper chamber with two newel stairs. It would not be surprising if the pilgrims to Walsingham were similarly marshalled up one staircase and down another, especially since the typical twelfth-century house (which one may presume Richelde to have copied) would be of two storeys, with the upper one the main one. That the building at Walsingham was of such a type is borne out by the only representation of it known to the writer, the small but interesting one given by two pilgrims' badges now in the King's Lynn Museum.[3] These depict clearly if conventionally a gable end of a house. It has two storeys, in the lower of which is a door whilst in the middle of the upper floor is shown a small representation of Our Lady seated with the Holy Child. The amount of detail feasible on a small badge of this kind is clearly strictly limited, but the representation of the statue is very similar to that on the seal of the priory

[1] Verses 10 and 13 of the Pynson ballad are the main authority for this.
[2] G. E. Street, *Gothic Architecture in Spain* (2nd ed. 1869), 169.
[3] See Plate 9 (*c*) and (*d*) and pp. 119–20 below.

—notably in the position of the sceptre and the Holy Child, as well as the chair—and the writer has very little doubt that this is intended as a simple souvenir of the Holy House and Statue of Our Lady of Walsingham. There were originally no less than four badges of the same or very similar type in the King's Lynn Museum amongst the few dozen badges in the collection, and the presence of so many of this kind in a smallish collection increases the likelihood of their being of Walsingham origin. Moreover it is significant that parts of two other versions of this design are to be found in the British Museum collection.

Erasmus does, happily, give us an invaluable glimpse of the interior of this inner chapel. Devotees were admitted 'on each side by a narrow little door. The light is small, scarcely any but from the wax lights. A most grateful fragrance meets the nostrils...,[1] when you look in you would say it was a mansion of the saints, so much does it glitter on all sides with jewels, gold and silver...,[2] in the inner chapel which I have described as the shrine of the Holy Virgin one canon attends the altar.'[3] Of the statue we are told only that it was 'a small image...of no extraordinary size, material or workmanship'[4] and 'stood in the dark at the right side of the altar'.[5] Erasmus goes on to give a brief glimpse of the treasures. 'He [the guide] then exhibited gold and silver statues and...added the weight of each, its value and the name of the donor..., and at the same time he drew forth from the altar itself a world of admirable things,[6] the individual articles of which if I were to

---

[1] Nichols, 13. [2] *Ibid.* [3] *Ibid.* 14.
[4] *Peregrinatio*, 356 = Nichols, 33, 'ostenditur imaguncula, nec magnitudine, nec materia, nec opere praecellens, sed virtute pollens'.
[5] Nichols, 24. [6] The larger offerings were preserved, *idem*, 12.

THE CHAPEL OF OUR LADY

proceed to describe, the day would not suffice for the tale.'[1]

On the outer building Erasmus is much less explicit, and only from the spade can we hope to learn much more about it. From Erasmus's remark that it was 'exposed on all sides', and from the steps found by the excavators,[2] it is likely that the building stood clear of the conventual church and was not built against it. Puzzling at first sight is his remark that the building was 'draughty with open doors and open windows'.[3] But Waterton very rightly suggests that, in view of the great concourse of pilgrims in the chapel, it may well have been found advisable to dispense with doors to its entrances.[4] Whilst it is to be noted that, by a curious chance, the time of Erasmus's visit to Walsingham probably coincided with a time at which new windows were being provided for the Lady chapel,[5] so it may well be that he arrived when the windows had lost their old, and not acquired their new, glass. It is probably because of this, and not because the building itself was incomplete, that Erasmus speaks of it elsewhere as 'unfinished' ('inabsolutus').[6]

To what period did these two buildings belong? As we have seen, William of Worcester in 1479 terms the larger one 'the new work'. This may well mean that the outer chapel was of recent construction, and, though the case of New College, Oxford reminds us of the dangers

---

[1] *Idem*, 37–8.   [2] Above, 97.
[3] 'Perflabilis, patentibus portis, patentibus fenestris', *Peregrinatio*, 345; Nichols (13) incorrectly renders 'perflabilis' as 'exposed'.
[4] *Op. cit.* 165.
[5] Above, 44, 47; the small chapel was probably of wood and would be too venerated to have modern windows inserted; in any case the considerable amount of money expended shows that it is the larger chapel that is involved.
[6] Nichols, 13.

that may lurk behind such appellation, such a date is not unlikely. If, as seems likely, the late fourteenth century saw the inauguration of an extensive rebuilding of the church and adjacent offices, it would seem natural to regard the building or rebuilding of this outer chapel as an integral part of the same plan. Clearly it would only be effected at a late stage in proceedings; and if, as is likely enough, Prior Snoring's expensive recurrence to Rome limited building activities in his time and thereafter, we would expect to find this scheme unfinished till the new century was well advanced, and this outer chapel of Our Lady, as a late part of the scheme, built in the mid fifteenth century. A letter from one William Yelverton to John Paston, written between 1444 and 1460,[1] has obscure references to 'Our Ladye's house at Walsingham' which it is conceivable may refer to some sort of building activity there (though this is by no means certain), and this would, of course, accord with William of Worcester's 'new work'. In the slype before mentioned are now preserved, *inter alia*, two fine diapered stone panels of late fifteenth- or early sixteenth-century date containing a crowned monogram which can be read as MARIA;[2] these are the sort of thing one might well expect to have been found during the clearing of the site of the Lady chapel in 1854, but it would be unwise to lean heavily on this possibility.

The little chapel itself which Erasmus saw must almost certainly have been that built by Richelde some four centuries before. The clue to this is given by the undoubted fact that it was thought fit to preserve it inside another chapel. The highly unusual nature of this step can scarcely be stressed too strongly. There were plenty of pilgrimages to relics of saints and statues of

[1] *Paston Letters*, 1, 62–3.   [2] Plate 7(*d*).

Our Lady in the Middle Ages, but very seldom was any sanctity attached to the building which contained them. As soon as money allowed, the old shrine would be pulled down and a more elaborate one in the modern manner erected. Only in the most exceptional cases was the primitive building, often small and inconvenient, retained down the centuries. Always when this was done it was because some exceptionally profound veneration restrained the ever present urge to rebuild.

No man dazzled contemporaries by his sanctity so much as St Francis of Assisi, and it was understandable that medieval man never dared to lay a hand on the chapel of St Damian where the saint passed his major spiritual crisis or the little chapel of Santa Maria degli Angeli near whose walls his soul left his pain-racked body. No English monastery had a longer past or one more closely interwoven with the saints of the Dark Ages than the abbey of Glastonbury, and it was equally understandable that there too the 'old church' should be jealously guarded when a wealthy and progressive age was building and rebuilding on the ground to the east of it. To cite another instance on a much smaller scale, the folk of Heysham, in building their post-Conquest church, did not pull down the little chapel of St Patrick, standing sturdily on the nearby cliff looking towards the saint's beloved Ireland.

Now Walsingham of course cannot be rightly classed with such shrines as these. It was beyond doubt a place of no special antiquity and its walls never nurtured a spectacular saint. One would have expected its history to follow that of other shrines of Our Lady, where a new generation might provide a more splendid shrine for the statue it so venerated, as, for example, the Florentines did, refashioning the Or San Michele in breath-taking beauty after the 'great and manifest miracles shown forth...by the picture of Holy Mary painted on a pilaster in the loggia'. But Walsingham differed essentially from this and others of its kind in that, whilst it was without doubt the greatest centre of Marian devotion in England, originally, at least, it owed its position to something more than the repute of its statue —the Holy House there.

Nothing is easier than to forget this, for the records of the priory's history are almost completely silent on this point. In the later Middle Ages it was primarily the statue of Our Lady that attracted attention. As will have been noted, the records mention Our Lady often, the Holy House almost never; and there can be no doubt that in the fourteenth and fifteenth centuries the latter was regarded as largely the setting for the former and not as a place of pilgrimage in its own right, conjoined though thought of the two inevitably was. Yet it was the presence of the Holy House, and this alone, that differentiated Walsingham from other shrines of Our Lady, and the fact that the House was preserved down the centuries is a proof of the importance attached to it.

As we have seen, this importance was not due to antiquity or personal factors; it can only have sprung from the connexion of the House with Nazareth, and it is significant that brooches showing the Annunciation were an important element amongst the tokens pilgrims bought at Walsingham.[1] It is not easy to be sure of the nature of this Nazareth connexion, but, as we shall see, it was never characterized by the extravagances that marked late fifteenth-century legends regarding the House of Loretto.[2] If the writer is correct, the Holy House of Walsingham was built as a private chapel by a

[1] Below, 117-18. [2] Below, 105-6.

ORIGINAL SITE OF THE CHAPEL

pious lady who may well have heard first-hand news of Nazareth from her son. The crusades would have been impossible had it not been for a passionate devotion to the soil of the Holy Land, the intensity of which even the trained historian to-day finds difficult to visualize. Yet it is only if we comprehend this passionate devotion to the land of Our Lord that we come to be in a position to appreciate why it was that Richelde's little chapel was so scrupulously guarded down the centuries.

A final point in connexion with the chapel is worthy of consideration. Was Our Lady's chapel transferred to a fresh site west of the original one and, if so, why was this done? There was an obvious practical reason why this might happen later in the priory's history. As time went on, the growing flood of pilgrims to Walsingham and the ever mounting stock of their oblations must have created a serious practical problem in view of the smallness of the Holy House. It might well have seemed desirable to move the Holy House with its statue to a more convenient site and to house other relics in a chapel on the old site (for medieval man was most unwilling ever to allow the desecration of a site once hallowed). At the time of the Dissolution the chapel of Our Lady was in a highly suitable position which fits in clearly with the rebuilt church of Prior Snoring. On the other hand the only authority for any such removal is the Pynson ballad which, as we have noted, maintains that the change of site went back to the time of the foundation. Workmen failed to build the church on the first site, but found it constructed overnight by angelic hands on the second one, 200 feet away.[1] This legend will not stand very close comparison with that of the Holy House of Loretto, which spectacularly tells of a completed building being

[1] Below, 127.

moved hundreds of miles, but it is by no means impossible that there is some connexion between the two stories. For only in 1472 does the legend of the Holy House of Loretto first appear.[1] That it was known in England not long after is certain, for Abbot Beere of Glastonbury (1493–1524) 'cumming from his embassadrie out of Italie made a chapelle of our Lady de Loretta, joining to the north side of the body of the chirch'.[2] By this time the Pynson ballad had been written (it was printed 1496–9), and it is possible to argue that it reflects, albeit very dimly, one of the latest and wildest legends of medieval Italy. But it is equally possible to assign this account of the transference of the chapel to the foolish passion for the spectacular which dogs guide-books perennially, and was, in this instance, stimulated by the distortion of some trivial incident in process of time in an insufficiently educated society. It is significant of the unreliability of the whole matter that, as Waterton points out,[3] the measures of the two Holy Houses by no means correspond, that of Walsingham being about eight feet longer than that at Loretto. With so little evidence, one can do little more than guess whether there was any transference of the site of the Walsingham chapel and, if so, guess its nature. The writer would conjecture that the Holy House at Walsingham always occupied the same site, being enclosed by the mid fifteenth century at latest in a larger building, but that, perhaps in the fourteenth century, the chapel of St Laurence was built by the wells to house relics that could no longer be accommodated in the Holy House.

Outside of the area of the church and cloister little

[1] See *Catholic Encyclopedia* under 'Santa Casa'.
[2] J. Leland, *Itinerary in England* (ed. L. Toulmin Smith, 1907), I, 290.
[3] *Pietas Mariana Britannica*, 169.

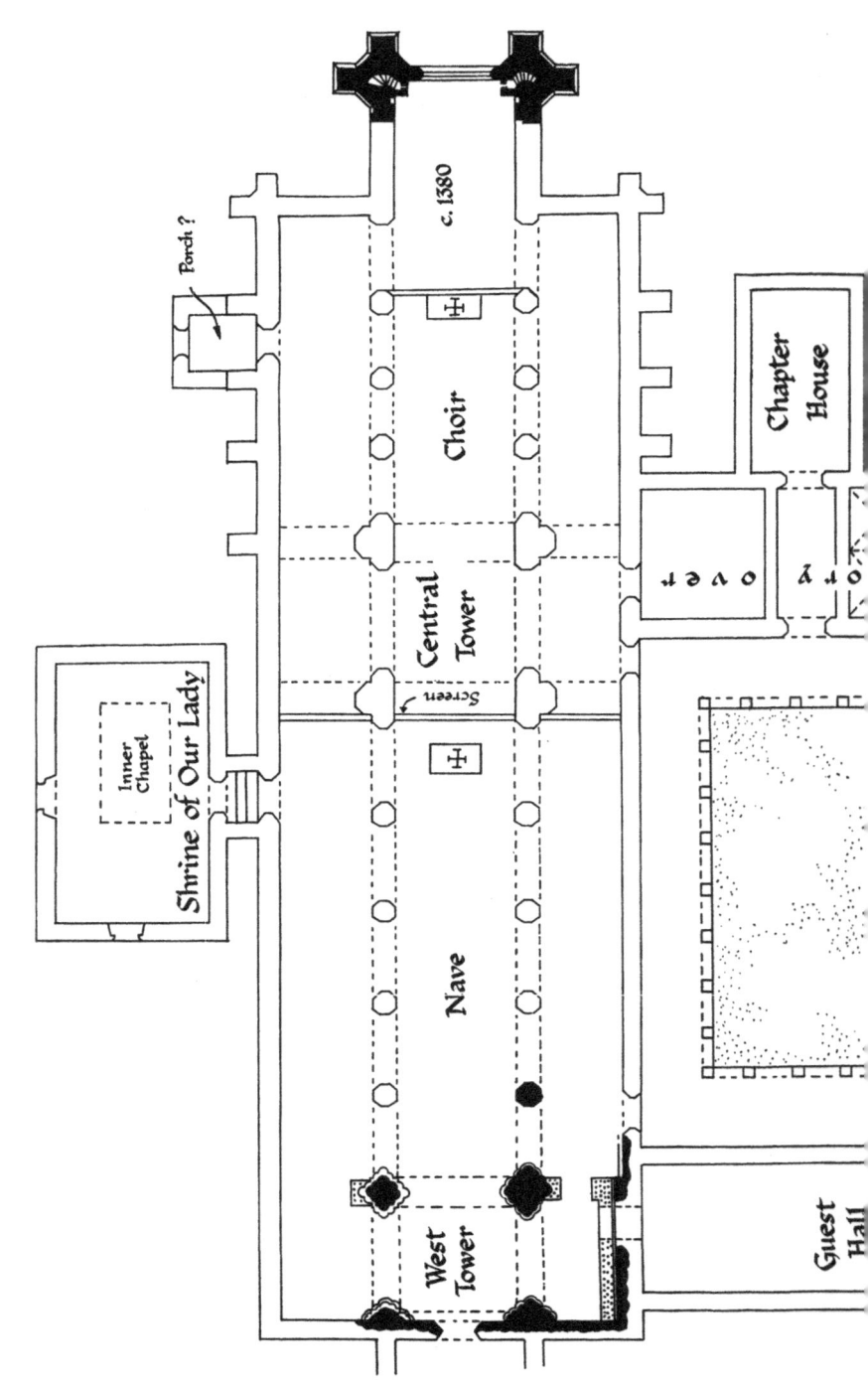

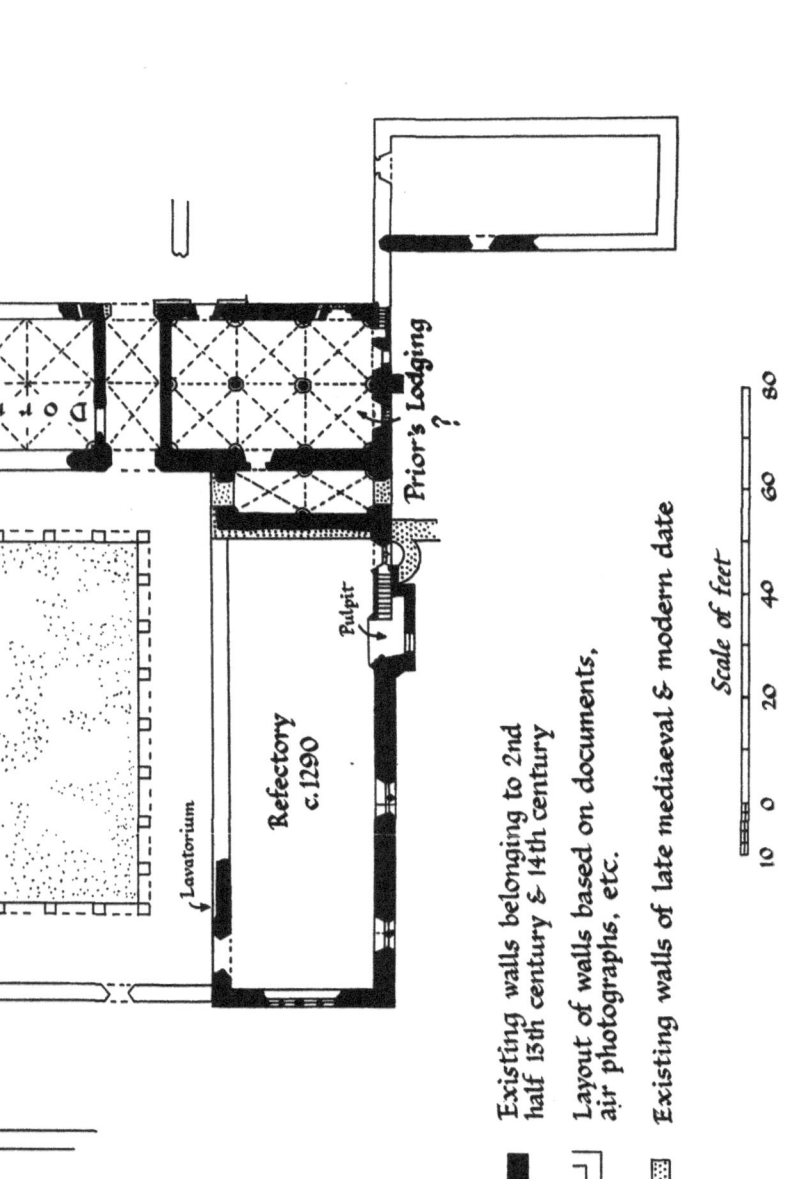

GROUND PLAN OF THE PRIORY

THE KNIGHT'S DOOR

remains of interest. But further mention should be made of the Knight's Door. It lies due north of the east end of the church at the point where the roads to Norwich and Knight Street meet. It has been badly damaged and radically restored and is now of little archaeological interest; the battlements are modern and the door has been remodelled and blocked up—but on the inner face are the remains of a pointed arch which may be of thirteenth-century date.

CHAPTER VI

MISCELLANEA: SEALS, STATUE, BADGES, ETC.

Two seals of the priory have survived. The earlier is known from a unique and rather indistinct impression in the British Museum.[1] It is assigned to the early thirteenth century in the catalogue but the design looks a little earlier. It is far from being large or attractive, contrasting most unfavourably, for example, with the handsome seal of West Acre Priory, Walsingham's neighbour.[2] In workmanship and general design it bears a very marked resemblance to a late twelfth-century seal from St Peter and St Paul's, Ipswich.[3] There are certain differences in architectural detail but the treatment of roofs, arcades and gable ends is very similar. A further striking resemblance—and a very unusual feature—is the insertion of signs of the house's dedication in the space between the roof line and the top margin. In the case of the Ipswich seal these consist of medallions having half-length busts representing St Peter and St Paul whilst the Walsingham seal has the letters M and (probably) W, presumably for 'Maria' and 'Walsingham'. The more elaborate belfry in the Ipswich seal and its more complex eastern limb (it has presbytery and sanctuary) show that we are not dealing with mass-produced wares, and suggest that it would be dangerous to take these representations as purely

---

[1] B.M., Add. Ch. 19,275; W. de G. Birch, *Catalogue of Seals in the British Museum* (1887) I, no. 4247, p. 788. (See Plate 6(a).)
[2] *Ibid.* no. 4294, p. 798.   [3] *Ibid.* no. 3317. *V.C.H. Suffolk*, 108.

SEALS OF THE PRIORY

conventional, restricted as their design must inevitably be by the scantiness of space. The legend of this Walsingham seal has almost completely gone, the 'SIG' of SIGILLUM alone surviving.

The second seal[1] is much better known, having been frequently reproduced.[2] It is a larger and much more elaborate piece of work, reflecting the increased importance of the priory and probably belonging to about the third quarter of the thirteenth century. The obverse shows a curious representation of the church. The cinquefoil and three openings with human heads set therein must not be taken too seriously, as they were one of the odd artistic conventions of the seals of this period[3] and can, *inter alia*, be paralleled on the seals of Walsingham's neighbours, Bromholm[4] and Norwich,[5] though the workmanship of the Walsingham seal is notably less expert. It seems that the building portrayed is the cruciform priory church with its central tower. We cannot be certain from what angle it was taken, but it is worth noting that the projecting portions are of equal length, in sharp distinction to their opposite numbers in the earlier Walsingham seal and that of St Peter and St Paul's, Ipswich. This suggests they are meant to represent the transepts of a cruciform church and that therefore the church is seen either from the east or the west; if the large arch in the centre is meant as a door it will be the west end portrayed, if a window, the east one. Mr John Harvey has pointed out to me that the

---

[1] *Catalogue of Seals in the Brit. Mus.* no. 4248, pp. 788–9; see Plate 6 (*c*) and (*d*).

[2] E.g. *Arch. Journ.* XIII, 127; a photograph of both obverse and reverse is given in *V.C.H., Norfolk*, II, 394 opp.

[3] See, for example, G. Pedrick, *Monastic Seals of the Thirteenth Century* (1902), photos 1, 3, 4, 37, 58, 75, 76.

[4] *Ibid.* no. 54.   [5] *Ibid.* nos. 65, 66.

transeptal pinnacles shown on the seal are found at Ely, Norwich, Gloucester and Wells and suggests that a realistic picture is intended. He makes the attractive suggestion that the seal represents a thirteenth-century church 'sketched symmetrically from the west before the completion of the nave'. This would accord with the western tower being known to have been built *c.* 1300, as the seal is rather earlier and one would expect the building of the nave to precede that of the tower.

The unlikelihood of the representation being the Holy House viewed from the north is supported by the position of the tower in the seal. The House itself is most unlikely to have had a tower, being too small for this and having no need of it, whilst a glance at the plan shows that the chapel does not lie directly in front of the crossing of the conventual church, so that it cannot well be argued that the seal shows the Holy House in the foreground with the tower of the church behind it.

Round the margin of the obverse is the inscription †SIGILLUM ECCLESIE BEATE MARIE DE WALSINGHAM† (The seal of the church of Blessed Mary of Walsingham). This is one of the very few English seals which also has an inscription round its rim; this reads: VIRGO PIA GENETRIX SIT NOBIS (Tender Virgin be our Mother). The reverse side of the seal shows Our Lady seated on a chair-like throne with the Holy Child on her left knee. Both have a nimbus and are shown full face. In her right hand Our Lady holds a sceptre fleur-de-lis. Curtains over the throne undulate round either side of it. Around the border is rather crudely cut AVE MARIA GRATIA PLEDA[1] DOMINUS TECUM.

Is this a representation of the famous statue of Our Lady of Walsingham? To answer this question it is

[1] *Sic.*

necessary to discover what grounds, if any, there are for the alternative solution that it is merely a conventional picture. One need not study more than a small proportion of the magnificent collection of medieval ecclesiastical seals in the British Museum before two points become clear. First, it is quite certain that at no period was there a completely stereotyped statue of Our Lady. From the late twelfth century the seals show a pronounced difference on points of detail. A good number show Our Lady seated, but many show her standing. In the former class there are notable divergences on points of detail such as the shape of the seat, the position of the sceptre and of the Holy Child and the angle of Our Lady's head. Thus there is no proof that the Walsingham representation is merely a stock piece; the contemporary variety in design makes it entirely feasible that the version on the seal was chosen for some special reason, such as its resemblance to the statue.

The second point to emerge is that, whilst the great proportion of seals of Our Lady examined differ significantly from that of Walsingham, there are a few which resemble it very closely. We must, of course, make all allowances for the fact that the Walsingham seal was designed in a good deal grander manner than was usual. The elaborate back to the chair and the complicated curtains have not been paralleled in any comparable English seals yet examined by the writer. But this should not prevent our recognizing that the essential details of the Walsingham representation of Our Lady and the Holy Child can be exactly matched elsewhere. Thus the small thirteenth-century seal of the Cistercian nunnery of Wykeham (Yorkshire)[1] and that of the Gilbertine house of Alvingham of the same period[2]

[1] B.M. Catalogue, no. 4377.   [2] *Ibid.* no. 2556.

do not differ from it in any essential trait; the rather crude seal of Luffield[1] resembles it quite closely in general design if not in treatment and that of Fineshade has also certain resemblances.[2] But the most remarkable parallel that the writer has so far located comes, not from England, but from France. Amongst the British Museum collection of medieval pilgrim badges is one evidently copied from a handsome twelfth-century seal of the famous French pilgrimage centre of Our Lady of Rocamadour,[3] and the Musée de Cluny at Paris has several similar examples. The likeness between this statue and that on the Walsingham seal is very remarkable, extending to every major detail except the chair which has no back in the Rocamadour badge.[4] The English seals are all thirteenth-century, except the Rocamadour one which is somewhat earlier. In our present state of knowledge it would be unwise to dogmatize as to whether the connexion between the two was direct or indirect, though it does not seem unlikely that Walsingham should copy Rocamadour.

The evidence so far has dealt with the similarity of seals and, in view of the paucity of English medieval statues of Our Lady, one cannot be certain whether in general a seal was of the same design as a monastery's statue of Our Lady or whether the two were different or whether (as the writer believes) the similarity existed in some cases.

But the case of Walsingham is further aided by the evidence of pilgrim brooches and ampouls from medieval England. So far as the writer has discovered these fall

[1] B.M. Catalogue, no. 3584; *V.C.H. Northants*, II, 136 opp.
[2] *Ibid.*
[3] Plate 6 (*b*).
[4] A similar high-backed chair is found in the statue of Notre-Dame Siège de la Sagesse at Ways (Belgium), originally at Mousty.

into five classes,[1] of which two are here relevant as portraying Our Lady. It is unfortunate that these badges have comparatively seldom got an inscription to identify their place of origin. But in the very interesting collection at King's Lynn Museum are several which portray Our Lady in a very similar manner to that of the seal. Though it is not absolutely certain that these badges are to be connected with Walsingham, it is at least extremely likely, seeing that they almost all came from a town which was so near Walsingham and a major centre for pilgrims to it. Our Lady is shown seated with a sceptre in her right hand that falls back on her shoulder; the Holy Child is on her left knee, both figures being shown full face. Perhaps because of shortage of space, the back of the chair is not shown, but in every other major point of design these badges agree with the representation on the seal.[2] It should be noted that several examples of this were also found at Lynn;[3] there are one or two similar ones in a collection in the British Museum.[4] Though the Walsingham provenance of these badges cannot be completely proved, it is much more likely than any other. We have no reason to think that any other statue of Our Lady in the south was important enough to warrant the manufacture of this sort of token on a big scale and, though the statue of Our Lady of Doncaster may have resembled that of Our Lady of Walsingham,[5] it was of very much less importance and very much less likely to be visited from London (where most of the British Museum badges were found).

Another type of brooch seems to the writer to clinch the matter—that already referred to as depicting a

---

[1] See below, 117–21. [2] Plate 9. [3] Plate 9 (b) and (d).
[4] Below, 119. [5] Below, 116.

similar statue of Our Lady on the first floor of a gabled house.[1] Here again Our Lady is shown seated with the Holy Child on her left and a sceptre resting on her right shoulder, exactly as on the seal. And, in view of what we have seen of the history of the shrine, the conjunction of this with the representation of the House makes the conclusion all but inescapable, that this represents the chapel and statue of Our Lady of Walsingham.

Thus there is, on the whole, adequate reason to believe that the picture of Our Lady and the Holy Child depicted elaborately on the later seal of Walsingham Priory and more simply on the brooches at King's Lynn and London is meant to be a representation of the famous statue there. (It is perhaps significant of the importance of the statue in the eyes of the designer of the great Walsingham seal that he devoted almost all available space to it, eliminating the elaborate tracery and praying priors so often found in similar seals of the period.)

A manuscript in the College of Arms of *c.* 1510 records the arms of the priory of Walsingham as *Argent on a cross sable 5 lilies slipped argent,* that is to say a silver ground with a black cross on which were five lilies,[2] and these are the arms of the priory shown on a shield of glass impaling the arms of Prior Vowell, found in the Abbey House and now in the parish church.[3] Taylor ascribes two other coats to the priory, (i) *argent on a cross sable, five billets of the first,* (ii) *argent on a cross quarterly pierced sable, a tree erased vert.*[4]

---

[1] Above, 99–100.

[2] MS. L. Lo, fo. 68; I am indebted to Mr A. R. Wagner, Richmond Herald, for this reference.

[3] Harrod, *op. cit.* 155.   [4] R. Taylor, *Index Monasticus* (1821), 26.

MANUSCRIPTS FROM THE PRIORY

Four manuscripts from the priory are known to have survived, apart from the cartulary.[1] Much the finest is a volume of a twelfth-century Bible now MS. 22 in the Chester Beattie collection.[2] It comprises the books from Genesis to Ruth and has attractive illuminations, some of which are reproduced in the *Catalogue*. At the front are three pages of quite minor rents which were privately printed by Sir Thomas Phillipps who once owned the manuscript;[3] on a fly-leaf, amongst small additions, is a drawing of a church tower with *Chapel Sancte Crucis*,[4] written round it. MS. 59 in the library of Keble College, Oxford, is half a fine breviary[5] from Walsingham; a very poor and inaccurate account of it is given in *Norfolk Archaeology*,[6] where the writer makes misleading use of what he failed to recognize was the Rule of St Augustine. The manuscript belongs to the fifteenth century and opens with the Rule of St Augustine arranged for reading by the days of the week followed by half a breviary; it concludes with some small liturgical miscellanea amongst which are prayers to St Dorothy and part of an office of St Richard of Chichester. Some of the illumination is attractive, without being of the highest class. Sloane MS. 1933 in the British Museum is a collection of medical treatises, mostly of the thirteenth and fourteenth centuries, which came from Walsingham, and Mr W. A. Pantin of Oriel College, Oxford, owns a small collection of prayers once in the possession of Prior Vowell. John

[1] N. R. Ker, *Medieval Libraries of Great Britain* (1941), 107.
[2] See E. G. Millar, *Catalogue of the Library of A. Chester Beattie, Collection of Western Manuscripts* (Oxford Univ. Press, 1927), I, 84–8.
[3] MS. 4769: Mr A. N. L. Munby has kindly pointed this out to me.
[4] *Sic.*
[5] I am obliged to Fr L. Boyle, O.P., for information regarding this manuscript.   [6] VIII, 51–6.

Leland notes that in the library of the priory were 'Gervasius super Psalterium, Joannes Capgravus, frater Augustinensis de Lino, super libros regum ad Joannem, episcopum Assavensem. Quod in regnorum libris'.[1]

The badges connected with the medieval shrine of Walsingham fall into two classes, brooches (secured by a pin and clasp like their modern successors) and ampouls or small hollow flasks which evidently contained water and had normally two small perforated lugs by which they could be sewn on a hat or garment. Though some are of pewter or brass, normally both types were made of lead and for this reason have seldom survived undamaged. No systematic study of English medieval pilgrim badges has been made.[2] The following paragraphs are based on the author's examination of the London collections of the British Museum, London Museum and Guildhall, and the local collections at Cambridge, Dunwich, Ipswich, King's Lynn, Norwich and Oxford, and make no claim to be exhaustive.

The larger of the two classes are the BROOCHES. Most of these have no indication of their place of origin, only a very few being inscribed; and in view of the popularity of other shrines of Our Lady, such as those at Ipswich, Sudbury and Doncaster, it is clearly most unwise to assume that English badges depicting Our Lady must necessarily have come from Walsingham.[3] Those which

---

[1] *Collectanea* (ed. T. Hearne), IV, 29.

[2] The best notice and bibliography of the English badges is that given by J. B. Ward-Perkins in the *Medieval Catalogue of the London Museum* (1940), 254–64.

[3] For a damaged badge from Doncaster see Plate 9 (*h*). We have a reference to these brooches in a letter from one Elizabeth Newhouse who wrote to her son: 'for a token, I send you a Walsynggam brooch' (*L. and P.* Addenda (i), no. 29).

we can assign to Walsingham with complete or reasonable confidence fall into three groups:

TYPE 1. *The Annunciation*

These all display Our Lady and the Archangel Gabriel with the usual lily-pot between. Four designs of this are certainly from Walsingham.

(a) A circular brooch with the Annunciation set within a circle which in turn is within a six-pointed star having three dots on each space between the points. (Part of a mould for making these was found near the churchyard of Little Walsingham in the last century and is now in the Castle Museum, Norwich.[1])

(b) The same design set on a broad arrow. (A cast for this is on the reverse side of that just mentioned.)

(c) An oblong brooch with the Annunciation enclosed in a frame that at the bottom is inscribed 'Walsingham'. (No original of this has been located but a cast of one has been described.[2]) Several others may provisionally be assigned to Walsingham.

(d) An unpierced circular badge inscribed 'Walsygham' below the Annunciation scene (there is a replica in St Peter Hungate Museum, Norwich, no. 26/52, from an original (now lost) found in the church of St Michael at Pleas, Norwich).

Among others possibly from here are:

(e) A small square brooch, uninscribed (Cambridge Museum, 22.781, from Norfolk; and King's Lynn);[3] the

[1] Described and illustrated in *Norfolk Archaeology*, IX (1884), 19–21.
[2] *Arch. Journ.* XIII, 133.
[3] Plate 9(g). It would appear that most of the pilgrim badges now in the King's Lynn Museum were originally collected by Mr Thomas Pung of King's Lynn who used to give boys coppers for procuring them in the (then open) Mill Fleet at Lynn. This collection was damaged in the 1939–45 war but a series of photographs of it had been taken in 1912. These are now in the possession of Mr H. L. Bradfer-Lawrence, F.S.A.,

Mill Fleet collection originally included several examples of this.

(f) A larger version of the above (British Museum;[1] one in the Mill Fleet collection, now lost, may have been from the same mould).

(g) A small representation within a circle, from which radiate projecting knobs (Cambridge Museum, 22.781).[2]

(h) A very large representation in a frame with an ogee arch supported by shafts with crocketed pinnacles; on the scroll is crudely inscribed ECCE ANC(I)L AVE MARIA (London Museum).[3]

(i) A medium-sized rectangular brooch (London, Guildhall Museum)[4] similar to (c) but uninscribed and having projecting points not unlike (g).

TYPE 2. *The Virgin and Child*

All are uninscribed, but it seems to the writer that examples showing a substantial resemblance to the statue depicted on the thirteenth-century seal of Walsingham and found in southern England may reasonably be assigned to the priory. This assumption is strengthened by the fact that two of the four surviving examples which agree exactly with the seal in showing Our Lady seated with the sceptre fleur-de-lis on her right shoulder and the Holy Child to the left[5] have been

who has kindly allowed me to utilize them and informed me of the history of the collection. The original collection is hereafter referred to as the Mill Fleet collection.

[1] Plate 8(a).

[2] This is from Norfolk and may be identical with that illustrated in *Norfolk Archaeology*, IX, 24 opp. especially since a broken brooch in the same museum closely resembles that illustrated in the same plate.

[3] Illustrated in London Museum, *Medieval Catalogue*, pl. LXIX, no. 14 (A 17216).

[4] Plate 8(b).

[5] I have rejected a number of the badges of Our Lady in the London Museum, as not having these characteristics.

found at King's Lynn, the nearest port to Walsingham; only one of the following, however, shows the seat having a back, as on the seal.

(a) A fine, large badge with the statue in a frame which has a three-sided canopy with ramparts and pinnacles (King's Lynn).[1]

(b) A small circular brooch containing the statue (King's Lynn).

Several others have been noted which may possibly have originated from Walsingham:

(c) A crude rectangular brooch with a border of chevrons and dots (British Museum).[2]

(d) A damaged, middle-sized brooch, perhaps originally of rectangular design, which depicts the (not unusual) bulges on the arms of the chair shown in the Walsingham seal[3] so that it may belong to the priory (British Museum).

(e) A brooch in London, Guildhall Museum,[4] has a figure not unlike the Walsingham one.

But brooches of this class cannot generally be assigned to a particular shrine with any degree of confidence.

TYPE 3. *The Holy House with a statue of Our Lady and the Holy Child similar to that of Type 2*

(a) The House is shown as a gable end and has two storeys with the statue in the middle of the upper floor and a pointed door immediately below, on the ground-floor, with pierced quatrefoil panels on either side of it. (Two examples probably from the same mould in the King's Lynn Museum[5] and (b) and (c), two similar but

---

[1] Plate 9(f).
[2] No. 56.7, 1.2060.
[3] *Ibid.* no. 98, 7–20, 5 (? from Coventry).
[4] No. 8693.
[5] Plate 9(c) and (d). The Mill Fleet collection had a third example.

MISCELLANEA

slightly different ones, formerly existed in the same collection.[1]) This design is technically unsatisfactory as the outer portions were not very strongly attached to the centre one and tended to break off. One side has done this in three of the examples noted above. In the British Museum are (*d*) and (*e*), what are almost certainly the right and left sides of two larger but closely allied versions of this design, essentially similar in general design to the King's Lynn examples but differing from them and each other in detail.[2] In the London Museum is an intriguing badge showing what appears to be the lengthwise view of a Romanesque building of two storeys; it is possible that this is a representation of the Holy House of Walsingham.[3]

The brooches cannot be dated with any certainty. They are unlikely to be earlier than the fourteenth century and such architectural details as they have look a century later.

The AMPOULS or miniature flasks are a clearly distinct type of souvenir and have perforated lugs to enable them to be sewn on to clothing. As is well known they were early found at Compostella. The following types may probably be connected with Walsingham.

TYPE I. *Flasks marked with a capital W*[4]

(*a*) One side of the body of the flask formed in the shape of a cockle shell, the other having a crowned W on a hatched background (found at Fincham and in 1922 'in the possession of Miss Barsham'; present

---

[1] Plate 9 (*a*) and (*b*).   [2] Plate 8 (*c*) and (*e*).

[3] Illustrated in London Museum *Medieval Catalogue*, LXXII, no. 50 (A 20809).

[4] No other English shrine of importance had this initial.

whereabouts unknown).[1] This corresponds except in minor details to the following (b).

(b) One illustrated by Lee Warner,[2] similar to (a), though here the letter has a plain background (Cirencester).

(c) Another 'marked with the crowned W found at Dunwich'.[3]

(d) One with a plain W at the bottom of one side, with a vertical ridge down the length of this side (Ipswich Museum, R 1920/74/47).

(e) Similar to (d) but slightly smaller (Ipswich Museum, R1935/65/55 A1).

TYPE 2. *Flasks having a Crown*

The crown occurs in the later Middle Ages as an emblem of Our Lady, and is found above her monogram at Walsingham.[4]

(a) A flask having on one side a cross within a circle and on the other a crown surmounted by sets of three dots[5] on a hatched background, similar to 1 (a) above, so a Walsingham origin is not unlikely (Ashmolean Museum, Oxford, from Icklingham, Suffolk).

(b) A simpler crown on a plain background set in a circle (Ipswich Museum, R 1935/65/55 A2).

(c) Similar to (b) but larger and without a circle (Ipswich Museum, R 1935/65/98 B).

In the British Museum is a fine ampoul bearing on one side a representation of Our Lady and the Holy Child[6] (very similar to that shown on the later seal of Walsingham[7]) and found 'in the river Somme, Picardy'.

[1] Below, Plate 9(e) (from a photograph given to the author by Rev. J. F. Williams).   [2] *Arch. Journ.* XIII, 133.
[3] *Ibid.* illustrated in T. Gardner, *History of Dunwich* (1754), 66.
[4] Plate 7(d).   [5] Plate 9(i).
[6] Plate 8(d).   [7] Plate 6(d).

MISCELLANEA

As we have seen, this representation is similar to the seal of Our Lady of Rocamadour, so the ampoul may have come from there. But we have also seen that pilgrims from the Flanders area came to Walsingham, so that such a place of origin cannot be ruled out.

The dates of these ampouls cannot be fixed but they are likely to be coeval with the brooches.

The priory is found acquiring property near St George, Colegate, Norwich in 1298,[1] evidently with the view to having a house in the town. The house itself has been demolished but a very fine door from it has survived.[2] It was given to the Norwich Museums and at the time of writing is in Strangers' Hall, Norwich. It is inscribed: MARIA PLENA GRACIE MATER M̄IE / REMEMBYR WYLLYĀ LOWTH PRIOR XVIII and measures 6 feet 11 inches by 3 feet 2 inches. William Lowth occurs as the eighteenth prior in the cartulary list[3] and ruled from 1504 to 1514. Fragments of alabaster carvings found built in a barn at East Barsham[4] were said to have come from the priory but this is uncertain.

In the church of St Mary the Virgin, Wiggenhall, is preserved a fine lectern inscribed: ORATE PRO ANIMA FRATRIS ROBERTI BARNARD, GARDIANI DE WALSINGHAM.[5] This is said to have come from Walsingham, and the Norfolk Church Inventories for 1552 show that there were then two lecterns in the church of Little Walsingham.[6]

[1] *Calendar of Deeds relating to Norwich* (ed. W. Rye, 1903), 64, 67.
[2] Illustrated in Harrod, *op. cit.* 178. The door has resemblances to that of Thoresby College, King's Lynn.   [3] Below, Appendix II.
[4] *Norfolk Archaeology*, XI, 257–8, where reproductions are given.
[5] *Ibid.* XIX, 318; see also C. C. Oman, 'Medieval brass lecterns in England' in *Arch. Journ.* LXXXVII (1930), 118–49.
[6] *Norfolk Archaeology*, XXVIII (1945), 225.

THE WALSINGHAM LECTERN

This brother Robert Barnard has not been identified, since his name does not occur in the list of canons of the priory. He is very much more likely to have been one of the Franciscans of the friary at Walsingham. Dr J. R. H. Moorman has drawn my attention to a Friar Bernard who was Warden of the Franciscan friary at Norwich in the late fifteenth century and had been at Cambridge in 1466–7.[1] He may well be the donor of the lectern, especially since *Gardianus* was the word used for the head of a friary.

[1] *Cambridge University Grace Book A* (ed. S. M. Leathes, Cambridge, 1897), 62, 72.

APPENDIX I

THE PYNSON BALLAD

THE ballad given below occurs in what is apparently a unique copy now included in book 1254 of the Pepys Library, Magdalene College, Cambridge.[1] After claiming that the chapel was founded in 1061, it later remarks that pilgrimages to it had gone on 'four hundreth yere and more', thus suggesting that the ballad was composed in the late fifteenth century, a date likely enough on other grounds.

Its original printer was Richard Pynson and the fact that he should have included it among his works is a further hint of the popularity of the shrine in early Tudor times. I am greatly indebted to Mr G. D. Painter, Assistant Keeper in the Department of Printed Books in the British Museum, for the following note on the original edition of the ballad:

"Duff, *XV Century English Books* (p. 131) and *Printers of Westminster and London* (p. 64), puts it among the other undated books of 1496. As far as one can surmise without seeing the book his reasons may have been as follows:

(1) The book is in Pynson's type 6 and 7. The first dated use of 6 is 1496, of 7 January 1495. Both, however, were used together till 1500 and later, so this evidence only suggests that the book is of 1496 or later.

(2) The book contains Pynson's device no. 3 (McKerrow, *Printers' Devices 1485–1640*, no. 9, plates 9a, 9b). The first dated use was 1497 but it occurs in many of the undated group assigned to 1496. An indentation in the bottom border occurs at latest from May 1499....

[1] Original spelling has been kept, but capital letters and punctuation have been modernized.

THE PYNSON BALLAD

I should say that the accepted date is *c.* 1496, while the possible range would be from early 1496 to early 1499."

1

Of this chapell se here the fundacyon,
Bylded the yere of Crystes incarnacyon,
A thousande complete syxty and one,
The tyme of sent Edward kyng of this region.

2

Beholde and se, ye goostly[a] folkes all,
Which to this place haue deuocyon
Whan ye to Our Lady askynge socoure call
Desyrynge here hir helpe in your trybulacyon;
Of this hir chapell ye may se the fundacyon,
If ye wyll this table[b] ouerse[c] and rede
Howe by myracle it was founded in dede.

3

A noble wydowe, somtyme lady of this towne,
Called Rychold, in lyuynge full vertuous,
Desyred of Oure Lady a petycyowne
Hir to honoure with some werke bountyous,
This blyssed Virgin and Lady most gracyous
Graunted hir petycyon, as I shall after tell,
Unto hir worshyp to edefye this chapell.

4

In spyryte Our Lady to Nazareth hir led
And shewed hir the place where Gabryel hir grette:[d]
'Lo doughter, consyder' to hir Oure Lady sayde,
'Of thys place take thou suerly the mette,[e]
Another lyke thys at Walsyngham thou sette
Unto my laude and synguler honoure;
All that me seche[f] there shall fynde socoure,

[a] Devout, spiritual. Cf. stanza 16, ll. 4, 6.
[b] Tablet.   [c] Turn over.
[d] Greeted.   [e] Measurement.
[f] Beseech.

APPENDIX I

5

Where shall be hadde in a memoryall
The great ioy of my salutacyon,
Fyrste of my ioyes grounde and orygynall
Rote[a] of mankyndes gracyous redempcyon,
Whan Gabryell gaue to me relacyon[b]
To be a moder through humylyte,
And goddys sonne conceyue in virgynyte.'

6

This visyon shewed thryse to this deuout woman,
In mynde well she marked both length and brede;
She was full gladde and thanked Oure Lady than
Of hir great grace neuer destytute in nede.
This forsayd hous in haste she thought to spede,[c]
Called to hir artyfycers full wyse,
This chapell to forge as Our Lady dyd deuyse.

7

All this, a medewe[d] wete with dropes celestyall
And with syluer dewe sent from hye[e] adowne
Excepte tho tweyne places chosen aboue all
Where neyther moyster[f] ne dewe myght be fowne,[g]
This was the fyrste pronostycacyowne
Howe this our newe Nazareth here shold stande,
Bylded lyke the fyrste in the Holy Lande.

8

Whan it was al fourmed, than had she great doute
Where it shold be sette and in what maner place,[h]
In as moche as tweyne places were founde oute
Tokened with myracle of Our Ladyes grace;
That is to say, tweyne quadrates of egall[i] space
As the flees[j] of Gedeon in the wete beynge drye,
Assygned by myracle of holy mayde Marye.

[a] Root, cause.
[b] Announced to me.
[c] Accomplish successfully.
[d] Meadow.
[e] High.
[f] Moisture.
[g] Found.
[h] What kind of place.
[i] Equal.
[j] Fleece.

THE PYNSON BALLAD

9

The wydowe thought it most lykly of congruence
This house on the fyrste soyle to bylde and arere.[a]
Of this who lyste[b] to have experyence,[c]
A chapell of saynt Laurence standeth nowe there
Faste by tweyne wells, experyence doth thus lere,[d]
There she thought to have set this chapell
Which was begonne by Our Ladyes counsell.

10

The carpenters began to set the fundamente
This heuenly house to arere up on hye,
But sone their werkes shewed inconuenyente,[e]
For no pece with oder wolde agre with geometrye;
Than were they all sory and full of agonye
That they could nat ken[f] neyther mesure ne marke
To ioyne togyder their owne proper werke.

11

They went to reste and layde all thynge on syde,
As they on[g] their maystresse had a commaundement;
She thought Our Lady, that fyrste was hir gyde,
Wold conuey[h] this worke aftyr hir owne entent;
Hir meyny[i] to reste as for that nyght she sente
And prayed Our Lady with deuoute exclamacyon,
As she had begonne, to perfourme that habytacion.

12

All nyghte the wydowe permayninge[j] in this prayer,
Oure blyssed Lady with heuenly mynystrys,[k]
Hirsylfe beynge here chyef artyfycer,
Areryd this sayd house with aungellys haudys,[l]
And not only reyrd it but set it there it is,
That is, two hundred fote and more in dystaunce
From the fyrste place bokes make remembraunce.[m]

[a] To erect. [b] Wish. [c] To make inquiry.
[d] Teach. [e] Troublesome. [f] Understand.
[g] From. [h] Manage. [i] Household.
[j] Persisting. [k] Services, aids. [l] *Sic*, hands.
[m] Mention.

APPENDIX I

13

Erly whan the artyfycers cam to their trauayle[a]
Of this sayd chapell to have made an ende,
They founde eche parte conioyned sauns fayle[b]
Better than they coude conceyue it in mynde;
Thus eche man home agayne dyd wynde,
And this holy matrone thanked Oure Lady
Of hir great grace shewyd here specyally.

14

And syth[c] here Our Lady hath shewyd many myracle
Innumerable, nowe here for to expresse
To suche as visyte thys hir habytacle,[d]
Euer lyke newe to them that call hir in dystresse;
Four hundreth yere and more, the cronacle to[e] witnes,
Hath endured this notable pylgrymage,
Where grace is dayly shewyd to men of euery age.

15

Many seke[f] ben here cured by Our Ladyes myghte,
Dede[g] agayne reuyued, of this is no dought,
Lame made hole and blynde restored to syghte,
Maryners vexed with tempest safe to porte brought,
Defe, wounded and lunatyke that hyder haue sought,
And also lepers here recouered haue be
By Oure Ladyes grace of[h] their infyrmyte.

16

Folke that of fendys haue had acombraunce[i]
And of wycked spyrytes also moche vexacyon
Have here be delyuered from euery such chaunce,
And soules greatly vexed with gostely temptacion,
Lo, here the chyef solace agaynst all tribulacyon
To all that be seke, bodely or goostly,
Callynge to Oure Lady deuoutly.

[a] Work. [b] Without mistake. [c] Since.
[d] Abode; canopied niche. [e] As.
[f] Sick. [g] Dead. [h] From.
[i] Have been oppressed by fiends.

THE PYNSON BALLAD

17

Therfore euery pylgryme gyue your attendaunce[a]
Our Lady here to serue with humble affeccyon,
Your sylfe ye applye to do hir plesaunce,
Remembrynge the great ioye of hir Annunciacion,
Therwyth conceyuynge[b] this bryef compylacyon,
Though it halte in meter and eloquence,
It is here wryten to do hyr reuerence.

18

All lettred[c] that wyll have more intellygence
Of the fundacyon of this chapell here,
If you wyll aske kokes[d] shall you encence[e]
More clerely to understande this forsayd matere;
To you shall declare the cronyclere
All cyrcumstaunce by a noble processe[f]
Howe olde cronyclers of thys bere wytnesse.

19

O Englonde, great cause thou haste glad for to be,
Compared to the londe of promyssyon,[g]
Thou atteynest my[h] grace to stande in that degre
Through this gloryous Ladyes supportacyon,
To be called in euery realme and regyon
The holy lande, Oure Ladyes dowre;
Thus arte thou named of olde antyquyte.

20

And this is the cause, as it apereth by lyklynesse,
In the is belded[i] newe Nazareth, a mancyon
To the honoure of the heuenly empresse
And of hir moste gloryous salutacyon,
Chyef pryncypyll and grounde of oure saluacyon,
Whan Gabryell sayd at olde Nazereth 'Aue',
This ioy here dayly remembred for to be.

[a] Attention, care.
[b] Taking notice of.
[c] Literate (persons).
[d] *Sic.* Query 'folks'.
[e] Insense, enlighten.
[f] Narrative.
[g] Promise.
[h] *Sic.* Query 'by'.
[i] In thee is built.

APPENDIX I

21

O gracyous Lady, glory of Jerusalem,
Cypresse of Syon and Ioye of Israel,
Rose of Jeryco and Sterre of Bethleem,
O gloryous Lady, our askynge nat repell,
In mercy all wymen euer thou doste excell,
Therfore, blissed Lady, graunt thou thy great grace
To all that the[a] deuoutly visyte in this place,

                                                    Amen.

[a] Thee.

APPENDIX II

PRIORS OF WALSINGHAM

THE cartulary of the priory[1] contains a list of the priors from the time of the foundation down to the time of Prior Hugh Wells. No dates are noted, but the length of each priorate is given except in the case of the fifth and sixth priors, where the combined length of their periods of office is given (presumably because the writer did not know the year in which the second of them succeeded). A later hand has added the priorates of John Farewell and William Lowthe and the period of office of Thomas Hunt. The list has been used rather uncritically in *V.C.H. Norfolk*,[2] and is printed in translation by Harrod.[3] If Walsingham priory had been of royal foundation it would have been possible to check most, if not all, of the priorates from government records. As it is, the evidence from elsewhere is less full but is amply sufficient to show that the list is completely reliable except at a few points.

The priorates from 1313 onwards can almost all be exactly determined from the evidence of the medieval bishops' registers and one or two subsidiary sources (see list below), and it is pleasing to find that in almost every case the figures in the cartulary list are found to be exact. This enables us to fill in with some confidence the dates of the earlier priors where little other evidence survives. The fairly numerous datable references to priors of Walsingham found by the writer in other sources all

[1] See fo. 157ᵛ.   [2] II, 131.
[3] *Gleanings among the Castles and Convents of Norfolk*, 181–2.

APPENDIX II

fit in with the evidence of the cartulary list, giving further proof that it is substantially accurate. The list enables us to fix the foundation of the priory at 1153, which again fits in with the evidence provided elsewhere.[1] The entry for Thomas the twelfth prior does not agree with the excellent pattern. His priorate is given as ten years, though the bishops' registers show quite clearly that it lasted from 1349 until 1374.[2] The episcopal evidence is of first class quality and is borne out by the later entries, so one is bound to conclude that for some unknown reason the writer of the list went astray on this point. Thomas was succeeded by Prior Snoring who is said to have ruled for twenty-seven years. He probably succeeded in 1374 and we know that his removal was ordered in 1400. It may well have taken some time to effect this, so it is not impossible that he was still in office in the following year. If we do not assume this we must hold that this entry is a year out. There is a similar minor problem concerning Snoring's successor Hugh Wells, whose priorate is said to have lasted thirty-five years. His successor is known to have been elected in 1437, so if the cartulary is right Hugh took office in 1402, a year after we should have expected. But this lost year is not inexplicable; it is just possible that there were two longish vacancies before Hugh and his successor were elected. Thomas Hunt's dates (1437–74) fit in exactly with all the evidence, as do those of his successor John Farewell, whose date of death is known precisely. The length of the priorate of William Lowthe does not note his time as prior of West Acre. The name of the last prior of Walsingham, Richard Vowell, is not given in the cartulary list, but can be supplied from other sources.[3]

[1] Above, 4–7.   [2] Below, 133.   [3] Below, 134.

PRIORS OF WALSINGHAM

Appended to the cartulary list are two notes, one right and the other wrong. The earlier one declares that the Statute of Quia Emptores of 1290 was passed in the time of Prior Peter who died well before 1270; what lies behind this error is unknown. The later note records Prior Snoring's attempt to secure the conversion of the priory into an abbey; as we have seen, it fits in perfectly with what is known hereon from other sources.

Cott. MS. Nero E. VII fo. 157ᵛ

Data priorum istius ecclesie

Ab ingressu canonicorum in ecclesiam de Walsyngham usque ad obitum Radulphi prioris primi

1153–73	fluxerunt anni xx
1173–86	deinde Ricardus prior secundus vixit xiij annis
1186–1207	Alexander prior tercius vixit xxj annis
1207–54	Willemus prior quartus vixit xlvij annis
1254–70	{*Petrus prior quintus vixit et Alanus prior sextus} xvj annis
1270–9	Willemus prior septimus ix annis
1279–99	Johannes prior octavus xx annis
1299–1313	Philippus prior nonus xiiij annis
1313¹–35²	Walterus prior decimus xxij annis
1335²–49³	Symon prior undecimus xiiij annis
1349³–74⁴	Thomas duodecimus x annis
1374⁴–?1401⁵	†Johannes Snoryng tercius decimus xxvij annis
?1402–37⁶	Hugo Well xv⁷ xxxv annis

[1] In Norwich Epis. Reg. he is named de Wyghtone; I, fo. 55ʳ.

[2] *Ibid.* II fo. 75ʳ. Simon de Wyveton admitted on the death of Walter de Wygtone, the last prior.

[3] *Ibid.* IV, fo. 100. Thomas de Clare confirmed as prior after an irregular election following the death of the last prior Simon Steyn.

[4] *Ibid.* VI, fo. 26ᵛ/27ʳ. John de Noryngg. [*sic*] confirmed as prior, following the resignation of Thomas de Clare.   [5] Above, 32.

[6] As we have seen, the date of Hugh Wells's installation as prior has not been located but on 8 Oct. 1437, his successor was elected 'in capella sancti Thome infra precinctum prioratus' (*ibid.* X, fo. 11ʳ) on the death of Hugh.

[7] 'quartus decimus' deleted.

APPENDIX II

1437[1]–74 Thomas Hunt prior xvj[2] (xxxvij annis)
1474[3]–1503[4] Johannes Farewell prior xvijus (vixit xxix annis)
1504[5]–14[6] Willelmus Lowth prior (xviijus vixit in priore x annis et resignauit pro pensione et postea prior de Westacr. exiuit, Deus cum eo[7]
[1514[8]–38[9] Richard Vowell]

Marginal Notes

* *M^d quod Anno vj^{to} petri prioris factum fuit statutum Quia emptores terrarum.*

† *Memorandum quod Johannes Herford gessit officium et nomen prioris predicto domino Johanne Snoryng existente Rome in placito pro abbathia de prioratu fienda; sed dominus Henricus Spenser [?] episcopus Norwicensis cum maiori parte conuentus huic officium[?] restituit et sic totus labor predicti domini Johannis, licet multum sumptuosus erat, erat cassatus.*

[1] See p. 133, n. 6.
[2] End of original hand.
[3] *Ibid.* XII, fo. 41^r. John Farewell was elected prior on the death of Thomas Hunt, 24 October 1474.
[4] *C.P.R.* (1494–1509), 332.
[5] The date of his election is not certain but was after the date of the licence to elect 15 Sept. 1503 and before July 1504 (above, 51).
[6] Above, 53.   [7] End of cartulary list.
[8] Below, 140. He is evidently the Richard Vowell prior of Lees, who resigned at this time (*V.C.H. Essex*, II, 156), but may have been a canon of Walsingham originally. He is termed *M[agister]* (below, 140) and preached a Latin sermon at the Augustinian General Chapter of 1518 (*L. and P.* II. (2), Appendix 48).
[9] Above, 66.

APPENDIX III

CANONS OF WALSINGHAM

THE following list from the cartulary is of some interest and is of a type not often found. It seems to consist of the names of canons who tried their vocation at Walsingham priory from the late fourteenth to the early sixteenth century. 'Postea dimissus' indicates that the canon in question left before taking final vows, 'Jubileus' that he had been professed fifty years. Various references to the names are found elsewhere but it has not been thought necessary to specify these. A rapid comparison of this list with one of canons of Walsingham ordained by the bishops of Norwich (kindly furnished by Rev. J. F. Williams) does not make it quite clear if the cartulary list is complete. This question is much complicated by the fact that canons seem to have assumed the name of a place (presumably that from which they originated) instead of their surname, the former being used in the cartulary almost exclusively, whilst the latter occurs in the registers. The later entries and some of the additional entries are added in an early sixteenth-century hand. A slightly inaccurate translation of the list was given by Harrod.[1]

[1] *Gleanings among the Castles and Convents of Norfolk*, 182–8.

APPENDIX III

B.M. Nero E. vii fos. 173ᵛ–174ʳ

fo. 173ᵛ a

Memorandum quod anno domini millesimo ccclxxxiiij⁺⁰

[1374–?1401]

    Johannes Snoryng fuit prior de Walsygham [sic] xiijᵘˢ
    Johannes Ieryngham alias Waryn fuit supprior et principalis adiutor circa constructiones ecclesie nostre.
    Johannes Barsham canonicus
    Ricardus Burnham canonicus
    Willelmus Barsham canonicus
    Thomas Bedyngham canonicus
    Nicholas Barsham canonicus
    Simon Warham canonicus
    Thomas Walsham canonicus
    Thomas Lynne qui fieri fecit les Clowse et(?) manibus propriis adiuuabat artifices summi altaris

[1389–?]

    Johannes de Herford bonus medicus et prior xiiijᵘˢ
    Johannes Peynton canonicus
    Johannes Yermouth supprior qui fecit depingi tectum corporis ecclesie nostre et capellam sancti Nicholai cum tabula ibidem et murum australem gardini australis nomine Jubilei sui, cuius anima in pace quiescat.
    Johannes Bakton canonicus
    Johannes Elyngham canonicus
    Ricardus Wyghton canonicus
    Thomas Fornsete canonicus apostatavit ratione furti quod commisit et postea capellanus honoris effectus est.
    Thomas Gatele supprior qui in puericia sua submersus fuit in fonte beate marie et mortuus sed per miraculum beate marie ad vitam est restitutus.

[?1402–37]

    Hugo Welles prior xvᵐᵘˢ per cuius laborem manerium de Eggem. acquisitum fuit. Qui eciam fieri fecit magnam campanam et plura alia memoria digna.
    Thomas Parham canonicus postea dimissus

CANONS OF WALSINGHAM

Walterus Ebon. canonicus

Thomas Hilgrave canonicus deo devotus qui pluros [sic] libros scripsit.

Willelmus Salle canonicus qui de bonis cuiusdam de Buria plura expendit circa edificationem cancelle ecclesie parochialis de Walsyngham.

Willelmus Bale canonicus

Willelmus Bacheler supprior

Johannes Derham canonicus et postea prior de Cokesford

Nicholas Agges canonicus

Johannes Houghton canonicus qui obiit in pulpito in ecclesia omnium sanctorum de Walsingham magna.

Thomas Myldenhale canonicus et postea vicarius de Bedyngham sed infra quindenam reuersus claustralis mortuus est

Thomas Crakesheld alias Mason canonicus postea abbas de Creyke

[1437-74]

Thomas Hunte prior xvi^{us}

Johannes Stanhowe canonicus postea abbas de Creyke

Edwardus Stede canonicus postea dimissus

Jacobus Baconesthorp canonicus

Willelmus Chestany canonicus postea frater augustiniensis

Willelmus Lynne canonicus qui fieri fecit librariam

Johannes Leryngsete canonicus postea dimissus

Johannes Walsham canonicus postea dimissus

Alanus Itryngham canonicus postea dimissus

Willelmus Derham canonicus Jubileus deo devotus

Johannes Gresseham canonicus postea dimissus

fo. 173^{v}b

Robertus Norwiche canonicus

Ricardus Hylburghwurth canonicus alias Mundy

Willelmus Paryse supprior et in iure canonico bacularius

Willelmus Norman canonicus

Thomas Houghton canonicus

Johannes Walsyngham canonicus

APPENDIX III

Thomas Derham canonicus
Ricardus Burnham alias Palle canonicus postea prior de Westacre
Willelmus Sharyngton canonicus
Willelmus Framyngham [*sic*] canonicus postea dimissus
Johannes Aylesham canonicus
Johannes Geyste canonicus
Edmundus Waburn canonicus postea dimissus

[1474–1503]

Johannes Norwiche alias Farewell prior xvij^{us} et in iure pontificio licentiatus
Thomas Cranewurth canonicus
Robertus Lyng canonicus
Willelmus Walsyngham alias Sesely canonicus et in theologia bacularius
Jacobus Thornhegge supprior devotissimus
Johannes Aleyns canonicus
Thomas Congham canonicus
Henricus Myleham canonicus postea prior de Cokesford
Thomas Byrcham canonicus postea dimissus
Jacobus Hempstede canonicus
Willelmus Fakenham canonicus
Nicholas Lucas canonicus
Ricardus Gottes canonicus et postea prior de Flyccham
Alanus Aylesham canonicus
Thomas Byrnyngham canonicus et in theologia bacularius
Egidius Sharyngton canonicus in theologia bacularius et postea abbas de Creyke.
Ricardus Holkham canonicus
Ricardus Waterden canonicus
Edwardus Warham alias Ponyon canonicus, postea supprior et Jubileus
Ricardus Keteleston canonicus postea Rector de Sharyngton
Johannes Grome canonicus
Thomas Grymston canonicus postea prior Montegaudii deus cum eo

CANONS OF WALSINGHAM

Henricus Burnham alias Cosyne canonicus
Nicholas Starman alias Sharyngton canonicus
Thomas Bynham canonicus postea prior de Hempton
Johannes Walsyngham alias Dyx canonicus
Thomas Creyke alias Hoker postea dimissus, deus cum eo

[1504–14]

Willelmus Lowthe canonicus, postea prior xviij et postea prior de Westaker per resignacionem
Willelmus Houghton canonicus
Cristoforus Barsham alias Warde canonicus
Robertus Parker alias Walsingham canonicus
Thomas Styffekey canonicus qui obiit apud London
Nicholas Ashehill canonicus
Willelmus Norwyche canonicus
Edmundus Feltwell canonicus[1]
Robertus Keteleston canonicus postea dimissus
Ricardus Swyneshed canonicus generosus
Thomas Lynne canonicus
Dionisius Talbotte canonicus et non professus
Thomas Walsyngham alias Lowthe canonicus postea prior de Thetford
Willelmus Walsyngham alias Giles canonicus
Ricardus Dokkyng alias Dolle canonicus
Edmundus Rynglonde nuper rector de Mulverton in artibus magister

fo. 174^r

Robertus Haale exiuit antequam erat professus

Willelmus Betts	diaconi simul professi
Ricardus Howys alias Brysley	et primi tempore
Thomas Ryngsted	Willelmi Lowth
Johannes Lowe	prioris anno domini
Willelmus Raase	1505 in festo
Johannes Pecke alias Aylsham	sanctorum Tiburtii
Johannes Watsune alias Clench-wardton	et Valeriani post pasca

[1] End of original hand.

APPENDIX III

Thomas Skeltune Colchest. postea dimissus
Thomas Wellys
Robertus Tylney alias Creke postea prior de Hempton
Thomas Ypswych canonicus ⎫
Willelmus Mileham canonicus postea
  canonicus de [blank]
David Norwich canonicus   Professi fuerunt
Nicholaus Cambryg canonicus postea   anno domini
  dimissus   M° cccccxj° et
Nicholaus Mileham canonicus postea   in festo sancte
  subprior   Dorothee
Robertus Salle canonicus po [sic]
Johannes Walsyngham alias Betts
  canonicus obiit aput Cantibrigiam ⎭

[1514–38]

Anno domini 1514. M. Vowel prior xix^{us}
D. Robertus Wilsey ⎱ canonici
Willelmus Gabbis   ⎰
Willelmus Rede alias Castylacr. ⎫
Simon Ovy postea dimissus   canonici exiuit [sic]
Thomas Albane   sine licencia
Johannes Harlowe ⎭
Ricardus Garnet
Johannes Quadryng
Johannes Lampley. solus professus, In die sancti Augustini doctoris. anno m° quingentesimo xxiij°. Postea ad Cantabrigiam missus et in jure divino bacularius et post supprior electus est et post annum unum capellanus episcopi Cantuariensis est cum magno labore effectus.

APPENDIX IV

THE SLIPPER CHAPEL

As is well known this is the name given to a small chapel at Houghton, about a mile and a half south-west of Little Walsingham. According to popular tradition this was the place where pilgrims to Walsingham took off their shoes before finishing their journey barefoot. As we have already noted, it is quite certain that some pilgrims to the shrine did visit it in this way, and the writer sees no objection to accepting the tradition as accurate, though it is to be admitted that we have no documentary evidence on the point. Indeed, so far next to nothing concerning the medieval history of the Slipper Chapel has been brought to light. The writer's attempts to discover any reference to its origin have been completely unsuccessful; in this connexion it is greatly to be regretted that no cartulary is known to exist from the priory of Horsham St Faith which owned the church of Houghton. The only available index to the massive unpublished registers of the medieval bishops of Norwich has not yielded anything; but it is far from complete, and it is possible that fuller examination of these magnificent volumes may ultimately prove fruitful.

It is, however, known that Walsingham Priory owned a little property in Houghton, that the present chapel stands on one of the principal routes to the shrine and was built at a time when the latter had acquired a national reputation. The architectural features of the chapel enable us to assign its erection to about the

APPENDIX IV

second quarter of the fourteenth century and it has been suggested that these features show similarities to the work at Ely Cathedral carried out by Alan of Walsingham (d. 1364).

After the Reformation it was put to various secular uses from which it was rescued by Miss Charlotte Boyd in 1894, after which it underwent a necessary but rather severe restoration and passed to Roman Catholic ownership. The chapel was reopened and a shrine of Our Lady erected there in 1934, being reconsecrated four years later.

BIBLIOGRAPHICAL NOTE

MAJOR original sources for the history of the priory of Walsingham are very scanty. The most important is the cartulary now in the British Museum (Cotton MS. Nero E vii) which has preserved the text of a great many charters of the house together with some interesting allied documents; it was drawn up about 1300 but has various later additions. Two folios of it are now in the Bodleian Library, Oxford (MS. Top. Norfolk b. 1). Almost all the original deeds of the priory seem to have vanished, though a few remain in the Bodleian, the British Museum and elsewhere. In the library of the Society of Antiquaries of London is an Account Roll of the cellarer of Walsingham for 1495–6 (MS. 622) and a few very trivial accounts are inserted in the Biblical volume from Walsingham, now MS. 22 in the Chester Beattie collection. I have not been able to examine more than cursorily the voluminous, unpublished registers of the medieval bishops of Norwich, but, to judge by the admittedly inadequate index of their contents, it seems unlikely that much important material for the history of Walsingham exists there. The only known episcopal visitations of Walsingham are those published by A. Jessop, *Visitations of the Diocese of Norwich 1492–1532* (Camden Soc. 1888). Otherwise the history of the priory has largely to be pieced together from isolated references in the principal government records and chronicles of medieval England many of which are conveniently listed in H.M. Stationery Office, Sectional List no. 24, and in C. Gross, *The Sources and Literature of English History...to about 1485* (1914).

BIBLIOGRAPHICAL NOTE

The Paston Letters (ed. J. Gairdner, 4 vols., 1900) have some useful references to Walsingham. Erasmus's *Colloquy on Pilgrimage* contains some valuable information about the shrine, but is to be used with caution; a translation of it with valuable notes was published by J. G. Nichols in 1875.

Little has been written on the house in the last hundred years. The excavations of 1853–4 were described by Rev. J. Lee Warner in *Archaeological Journal*, XIII (1856), pp. 115–34, with which should be compared the account of Walsingham in H. Harrod's *Gleanings among the Castles and Convents of Norfolk* (Norwich, 1857), pp. 154–97. Of later accounts, in many ways the most useful, despite its polemical character, is that in E. Waterton's *Pietas Mariana Britannica* (1879). The account of the priory in the *Victoria County History of Norfolk*, II, pp. 394–401, though not without use, is somewhat disappointing.

THE PLATES

PLATE 1

WALSINGHAM PRIORY, FROM THE ENGRAVING BY BUCK, 1738

PLATE 2

THE EAST END OF THE CHURCH

PLATE 3

(*a*) THE PRIORY FROM THE AIR

(*b*) ST LAURENCE'S CHAPEL

PLATE 4

(*a*) THE REFECTORY

(*b*) THE WELLS

PLATE 5

THE UNDERCROFT

PLATE 6

SEALS, ETC.

(a) First seal of Walsingham
(b) Badge of Our Lady of Rocamadour
(c) Later seal of Walsingham (obverse)
(d) Later seal of Walsingham (reverse)

PLATE 7

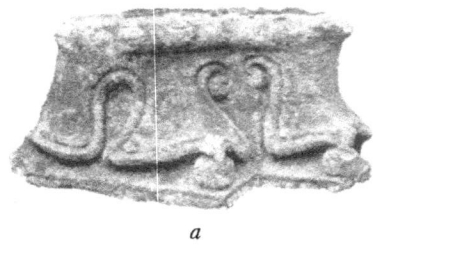

a b

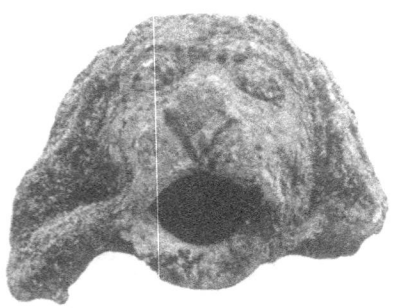

c d

ARCHITECTURAL DETAILS

(a) Capital (c. 1180) (b) Twin capitals (c. 1240)
(c) Gargoyle (c. 1400) (d) Stone panel (c. 1500)

PLATE 8

BADGES AND AMPULLA

(a) B.M., 91/4-18/25   (b) London, Guildhall Museum, 8689
(c) and (e) B.M., Hugo Collection (d) B.M., 60/9-7/3

(Natural size)

PLATE 9

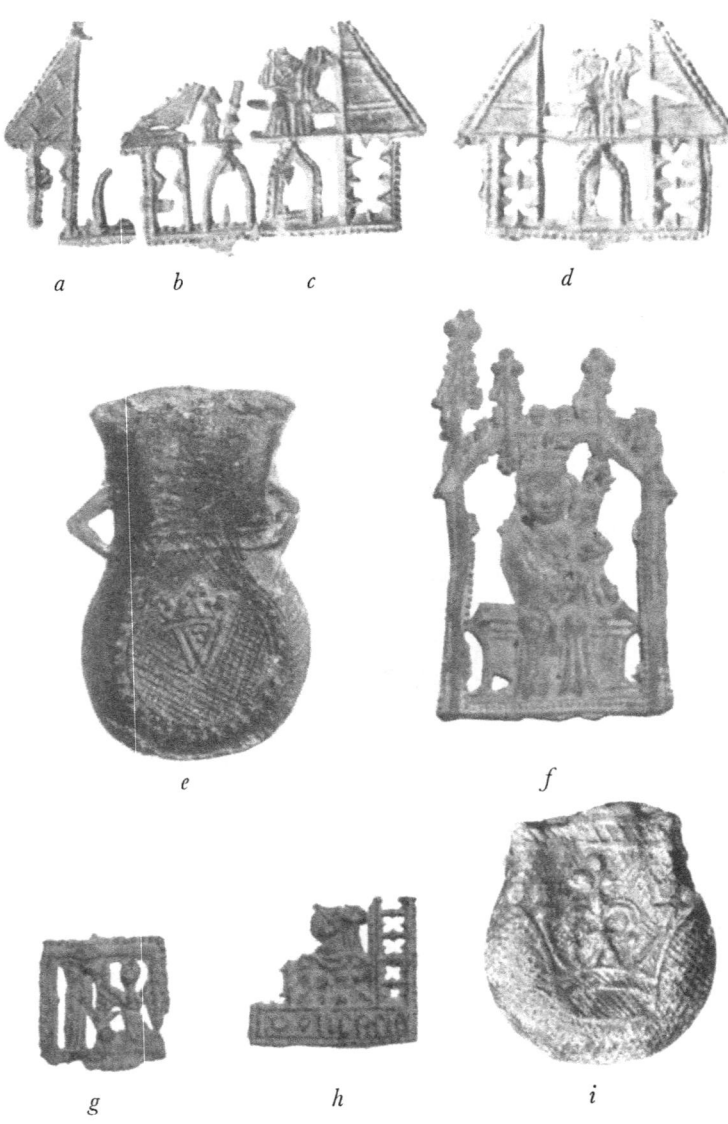

BADGES AND AMPULLAE

(*a*) and (*b*) Mill Fleet, King's Lynn (now lost); (*c*) and (*d*) King's Lynn Museum; (*e*) Present whereabouts and size unknown; (*f*), (*g*) and (*h*) King's Lynn Museum; (*i*) Oxford, Ashmolean Museum 1927/6409.

(Natural size)

INDEX

Abbey, proposal to make Walsingham an, 28f.
Abbey House, Walsingham, 71–2, 85, 86–8
Account Roll from Walsingham, 38, 51 n. 4
aid of 1235–6, 15
air photograph of Walsingham, 77
alabasters, possibly from Walsingham, 122
Alan, prior of Walsingham, 133
Alcock, John, bishop of Ely, 77
Alexander, prior of Walsingham, 133
Alfred, King, 3
Alvingham Priory, 111
ampouls from Walsingham, 120–2
Andrew, Lady Elizabeth, 37
Anglican shrine at Walsingham, 13 n. 3, 68
Anjou, duke of, 25
annals of the chapel of Walsingham, 11, 38
Antiquaries, Society of, London, 38 n. 4
arch near the wells at Walsingham, 73, 94–5
architectural history of Walsingham Priory, 71–7
Armagh, archbishop of, *see* Fitz-Ralph
Arthur, King, 3
Arthur, Master, 45
'Articles of Enquiry' concerning Walsingham, 60
Arundel, Thomas, archbishop of Canterbury, 32
Philip, earl of, 67

Badges, pilgrim, from Walsingham, 99–100, 112–14, 116–22

ballads on Walsingham, *see* poems on Walsingham, Pynson
banner, *see* standard
Barett, Anne, 47
Barnard, Robert, Franciscan, 122–3
Barnwell Priory, 56
Barsham, East, 122
Barsham, Miss, 120
Barton, Catherine, 46
Beck, hospital of, 16
Beckinton, *see* Beck
Bedingham, 60, 137
Beere, Richard, abbot of Glastonbury, 96, 106
Beyston, John, 46
Bible from Walsingham, 115
Bicester Priory, 11
Binham, Thomas, cellarer, 38
Binham Priory, 5, 49, 63
Bintree, 22
Black Death, 49
Blythburgh Priory, 16
Bond, A., 93
Book of Hours, in Cambridge University Library, 4
le Boucher, Gerard, 25
Bradfer-Lawrence, H. L., 117 n.
breviary from Walsingham, 115
Bricett Priory, 16
Bridlington Priory, 14, 56, 88
Brittany, John, duke of, 25
Britton, John, 72
de Brocas, Sir Bernard, 25
Bromholm Priory, 15 n. 4, 17, 20, 22, 27, 35, 109
brooches, Walsingham, 112–14, 116–20
Bruce, David, 25
Brutus, 3
Buckingham, dukes of, 35, 45
de Burgh, Hubert, 16 n. 1

INDEX

de Burghersh, Sir Bartholomew, 36
Bury St Edmunds Abbey, 7 n. 1, 20, 25, 44, 82
Butley Priory, 16, 78

Cabbokeswell, 13
Cambridge 42, 140 (*bis*)
canons of Walsingham Priory, *see* Gatele, Lynn, Yarmouth
  list of, 12, 75, 135–40
  number of, 50, 81 n.3
Cantaber, Prince, 3
Canterbury, 25 (*bis*), 44, 62, 81 n.3, 93
  archbishops of, *see* Arundel, Pecham, Reynolds, St Thomas
Capgrave, John, 11, 27, 38, 116
cartulary of Walsingham Priory, 4 *and passim*
Castle Acre Priory, 6
Caversham, Our Lady of, 37
chapel of Our Lady, Walsingham, 4, 12 f., 42, 55, 56, 63, 97 f., 125–30
Chapuys, 47
Charlemagne, 3
chasuble sent to Walsingham, 19
le Chaumpeneys, John, 22
Chester Beattie collection, 115
Cheyney, family of, 77
Chichester, St Richard of, *see* St Richard
Cirencester, 121
Clare, Lady, 36, 76
de Clare, Gilbert, earl of Gloucester, 16
  Roger, earl of Hereford, 5
  William, earl of Gloucester, 16
coat-of-arms of Walsingham Priory, 114
Colloquies of Erasmus, 47, 54
  see also *Peregrinatio religionis ergo*
'Common Place', the, 96
Compiègne, 25
Compostella, 11, 93, 99, 120
Cornish soldiers on pilgrimage, 46
Coxford priory, 10, 16, 59, 137, 138

Creake, abbey, 48, 137, 138
  South, 66
Crikyere, Thomas, 26–7
Cromwell, Thomas, 62, 66
crown, for the statue of Our Lady of Walsingham, 19

Daniel, Russian abbot, 13, 98
Domesday Book, 6
Doncaster, Our Lady of, 113, 116
Dudley, Edmund, 51, 52
Dunwich, 121

Ecopp, William, 37
Edward I, King, 19–21, 39–40, 60
Edward II, King, 24, 40, 60
Edward III, King, 24–5, 40
Edward IV, King, 34–5
Edwy, 10
Elizabeth, Queen, 44 n.4
Ely, bishops of, *see* Alcock, West
  cathedral of, 82
Empson, Sir Richard, 51, 52
Erasmus, Desiderius, 13, 47, 53 f., 61, 91, 96, 100, 101
excavations at Walsingham Priory, 72
executions at Walsingham, 64
Exeter, marquis of, 45

Fairs, at Bromholm, 17
  at Walsingham, 17–18, 19
Farewell, John, prior of Walsingham, 41, 51, 131, 132, 134, 138
Fastolf, Sir John, 34
de Fervaques, Geoffrey I, 5–6
  Geoffrey II, 4, 5, 6, 7, 10, 15
  Richelde, 4, 5, 6–7, 99, 102, 125–7
Fincham, 120
fire at Little Walsingham, 34
FitzRalph, Richard, archbishop of Armagh, 27
Flanders, count of, 21
flasks, *see* ampouls
Flitcham Priory, 41 n.6, 48, 59, 138

INDEX

Flodden Field, battle of, 44
Flour, Barnard, 44
Fraisthorpe, 14
Franciscan friary at Walsingham, 26, 90, 95, 122–3

Gabriel the archangel, statue of, 8, 13, 39
Galant, John, 64
gatehouse of Walsingham Priory, 78–9
Gatele, Thomas, subprior of Walsingham, 12, 136
Gaunt, John of, 25
Geoffrey, see de Fervaques
Gervasius, 116
Ghent, 35
gifts to the shrine of Walsingham, 35–40, 42–4
Glasgow Cathedral, 81
Glastonbury Abbey, 96, 103, 106
Gloucester, Gilbert, earl of, 16
William, earl of, 16
Gresham, Sir Richard, 66
Gysburghe (Gisborough), George, 63, 64

Halibred house, 77
Haly, John, 46
Harrod, Henry, 72
Harvey, J. H., 81, 99, 109–10
Hastings, Lady Catherine, 38
Hempton, priors of, 139, 140
Henry II, King, 17
Henry III, King, 17, 18–19
Henry V, King, 34
Henry VI, King, 34
Henry VII, King, 41–2
Henry VIII, King, 42–4, 59
Hereford, Roger, earl of, 5
Herford, John, prior of Walsingham, 31, 134, 136
Hertford jail, 26
Heslerton, 37
Heydon, Sir John, 64
Heysham, 103
Holy House, of Loretto, 94, 104, 105–6
of Nazareth, 7, 12, 13, 98, 125
of Walsingham, 7–8, 13, 55, 104–5, 106, 119–20, 125f.
Holy Milk, see relics at Walsingham Priory
Horsham St Faith, 141
de Houghton, William, 5 (*bis*)
Houlot, Thomas, canon of Walsingham, 49
Hull, church of Holy Trinity, 81
Hunt, Thomas, prior of Walsingham, 132, 133

Icklingham, 121
image of Edward I, 39
of Henry VII, 42
of Our Lady, see Caversham, Doncaster, Ipswich, statue of Our Lady of Walsingham
indulgence, granted to Walsingham, 77
inns, at Little Walsingham, burnt, 34
Ipswich, ampouls from, 121
Our Lady of, 46, 65, 116
priory of St Peter and St Paul, 16, 108
Isabella, Queen, 24, 25, 40

Jeryngham, John, 76, 136
Joan, Queen, 34
John, King, 17
prior of Walsingham, 133

Katherine of Aragon, Queen, 44
Keble College, Oxford, 115
Kemp, Margery, 34
King's Lynn, 113, 116, 117 and n. 3, 119, 120
Mill Fleet collection of badges, 117 and n.3
Knight's door, 57, 107

Lac sacrum, see relics at Walsingham Priory
Lancaster, Henry, duke of, 38
de Landa, Amanda, 25
Langland, William, 27

INDEX

Lapworth church, 99
lectern from Walsingham, 122
Lee Warner, Henry, 71–2
   Rev. J. 72, 121
Leland, John, 4 n. 1, 6, 116
library of Walsingham Priory, 76, 85, 137
Lincoln, bishop of, *see* Longland
   wills from, 46
Lindsay, Sir James, 25
Lollards, 27
London, bishop of, *see* Tunstall
Longland, John, bishop of Lincoln, 46
Loretto, *see* Holy House
Lowthe, William, prior of Walsingham, 52 f., 122, 131, 132, 134, 139
Luffield Priory, 112
Lynne, Thomas, canon of Walsingham, 76, 136

Magdalene College, Cambridge, 124
manuscripts from Walsingham Priory, 115–16
March, Edmund, earl of, 36
   Roger, earl of, 28, 29
market at Walsingham, 17
Marshall, John and Ellen, 60
Mauleverer, William, 37
Mileham, Nicholas, subprior of Walsingham, 64, 140
Michelham Priory, 88
de Montfort, Simon, 94
Moorman, J. R. H., 123
mortmain, licences in, 24, 40–1
Mountjoy, priors of, 48, 138
   priory of, 48

Nazareth, *see* Holy House
Newhouse, Elizabeth, 116 n. 3
Nicolls, Benedict, bishop of St David's, 36
Norfolk, duke of, 34
Norwich, bishops of, *see* Spenser, Henry; de Turbe, William
   cathedral priory of, 22, 109
   Colegate, house in, 122
   St Michael at Pleas, 117

Oak trees, gifts of, 18, 73
O'Reef, Thomas, 46
Oulton church, 16 n. 1

Painter, G. D., 124
Pantin, W. R., 115
Paston family, 34, 35, 42
Paston Letters, 33, 102
Pecham, John, archbishop of Canterbury, 23
Pecock, Reginald, 27
Pentney Priory, 16, 78
Peregrinatio religionis ergo, 47, 53 f.
Peter, prior of Walsingham, 133 (*bis*)
Peterborough, abbey of, 34
   abbot of, 34
Peterstone Priory, 48
Petre, Sir William, 66
Philip, prior of Walsingham, 133
Phillipps, Sir Thomas, 115
Piers the Plowman, Vision of, 27
pilgrim badges, *see* ampouls, badges, brooches
Pipe Rolls, 5, 6, 18
places of pilgrimage at Walsingham, 91–107
plan of Walsingham Priory, 74, 80, 81
poems on Walsingham, 67–8, 124–30
Ponte, William, 37
Praemunire, Statutes of, 33
prayers, book of, from Walsingham, 115
priors of Walsingham, *see* Farewell, John; Herford, John; Lowthe, William; Ralph; Snoring, John
   list of, 4, 131–4
Provisors, Statutes of, 33
Pynson, Richard, 4
Pynson ballad, 4, 6, 8, 94, 96, 105, 124, 124–30 (text)

INDEX

Queens, *see* Elizabeth, Isabella, Joan, Katherine of Aragon
Quia Emptores, Statute of, 133, 134

Ralph, prior of Walsingham, 10, 133
refectory of Walsingham Priory, 88–9
regular canons introduced at Walsingham, 4, 7, 9–11
relics, from the Holy Land, 56
at Walsingham Priory, 39–40, 55, 56, 60, 82, 91–2
Reynolds, Walter, archbishop of Canterbury, 35
Richard I, King, 17
Richard II, King, 25
Richard III, King, 38
Richard, prior of Walsingham, 133
Richelde, *see* de Fervaques
rising, Norfolk, 63–4
Rivers, Anthony, earl of, 37
Rogerson, Ralph, 63

St Anne, chapel of, at Walsingham, 76
St Benet's, Hulme, Abbey, 82
St David's, *see* Nicolls
St Dorothy, 115
St Laurence's chapel at Walsingham, 60, 80, 83, 91, 95, 106, 127
St Nicholas's chapel at Walsingham, 76, 136
St Osyth, priory of, 78
St Paul's Cathedral, London, 27
St Pol, Guy, count of, 25
St Richard of Chichester, 115
St Thomas of Canterbury, 25, 81, 93
schoolmasters, 50–1
Scrope, Lady Ann, 38
Lord John, 37
seals of Our Lady, 112
seals of Walsingham Priory, 73, 108–12

Sharington, 138
Simon, prior of Walsingham, 133
Slipper Chapel, Houghton, 26, 68, 141–2
Smith, John, 52, 53
Smyth, Richard, 46
Snoring, John, prior of Walsingham, 28f., 75–6, 132, 133, 134n., 136
Somme, river, 121
Southwell, Richard, 64 (*bis*)
Spalding, John, 46
Spelman, Henry, 43, 67
Spenser, Henry, bishop of Norwich, 30, 134n.
squints at Walsingham Priory, 86
standard, royal, offered at the shrine of Walsingham, 42
statue of Our Lady of Walsingham, 9, 39, 65 and n.8, 110f.
crown for the, 19. *See also* Gabriel
necklaces for, 43, 65
Stone, priory of, 11
Strange, Sir Roger, 47
Suffolk, William, earl of, 36
suppression of Walsingham Priory, 59–67
Surrey, John, earl of, 36
Sydney, Thomas, 66–7

Tank at Walsingham Priory, 93–4
tapers, *see* wax
Taxatio Ecclesiastica (1291), 22
Terra Vasta, Rowland of, 15
Thetford, prior of, 139
Thomas I, prior of Walsingham, 133
Thomas II, prior of Walsingham, 132, 133
de Tonge, Semari, 36
Townsend, Sir Roger, 64
treasury at Walsingham Priory, 53
treaty concluded at Walsingham, 21
Tunstall, Cuthbert, bishop of London, 46

INDEX

de Turbe, William, bishop of Norwich, 5

Urswick, Christopher, 42
university, regular canons at the, 51, 59
Uvedale, Sir John, 60
  Sir Thomas, 35, 76

Valor Ecclesiasticus (1535), 59–60
Vergil, Polydore, 41
visitations of Walsingham Priory, 49 f.
Vowell, Richard, prior of Walsingham, 59, 62, 64–5, 66, 114, 132, 134

Walsingham, Franciscan friary at, *see* Franciscan
  abbey, attempt to make the priory an, 28 f.
  account roll of, 38, 51 n.4
  air photograph, 77
  arch near the wells at, 73, 94–5
  architectural history of, 71–7
  bible from, 115
  breviary from, 115
  candles offered at, 19, 42, 43
  canons of, *see* canons
  capital of twelfth century at, 73
  cartulary of, 4 *and passim*
  chapter house of, 85
  cloister of, 85 f., 90
  coat-of-arms of, 114
  east end of church of, 82–3
  eastern range of, 85–8
  excavations at, 72
  foundation of, 3–11
  gargoyle at, 76
  gatehouse of, 78–9
  halibred house at, 77,
  high altar of, 76
  Holy House at, *see* Holy House
  Knight's door at, 57, 107
  library of, 76, 85, 137
  manuscripts from, 115–16
  pictures of, 71

  pilgrim badges of, *see* ampouls, badges, brooches
  poems on, 67–8, 124–30
  porch at, 83
  porter's lodge at, 80
  prior's apartments at, 88
  priors of, *see* priors
  priory church of, 80
  priory of Austin canons at, 4–5, 9, 16, 22
  refectory of, 88–9
  relics at, 39–40, 55, 56, 60, 82, 91–2
  sacristy at, 85
  St Anne's chapel at, 76
  St Laurence's chapel at, 60, 80, 83, 91, 95, 106, 127
  St Nicholas's chapel at, 76, 136
  St Thomas's chapel at, 77
  seals of, 73, 108–12
  shed over wells at, 55
  slype at, 87, 102
  squints at, 86
  statue of Our Lady at, *see* statue
  stone panel at, 102
  suppression of, 59–67
  tank near the wells at, 93–4
  towers of, 82, 84
  treasury of, 53
  undercroft of eastern range at, 86–7
  visitations of, 32, 49 f.
  wells at, 12, 92, 93, 94
  western range of, 89–90
  see also Abbey House, chapel of Our Lady, places of pilgrimage at Walsingham, Slipper Chapel
Walsingham, Thomas of, 27
Walter, prior of Walsingham, 133
Warwick, earl of, 34
  Isabel, countess of, 37
Waterton, E., 56, 57, 80, 101
wax, gifts of, 18
Wells, Hugh, prior of Walsingham, 131, 132, 133, 136
wells at Walsingham priory, 12, 92, 93, 94

INDEX

West, Nicholas, bishop of Ely, 45
West Acre Priory, 10, 16, 53, 108, 132, 138, 139
Wiggenhall St Mary, church of, 122
William, brother of King Henry II, 15
William I, prior of Walsingham, 133
William II, prior of Walsingham, 133
Williams, Rev. J. F., 121 n.
Winterton, fishermen of, 26

Witten Bouc, 35
Wolsey, Cardinal, 45, 46, 48, 58
Wolveton, Adam de, 27
Worcester, William of, 77–8, 97, 98, 101
Wormgay Priory, 16
Wykeham Priory, 111
Wymondham Priory, 82

Yarmouth, John, canon of Walsingham, 29, 76, 136
York, duke of, 34
   Elizabeth of, 42

For EU product safety concerns, contact us at Calle de José Abascal, 56–1°, 28003 Madrid, Spain or eugpsr@cambridge.org.

www.ingramcontent.com/pod-product-compliance
Lightning Source LLC
LaVergne TN
LVHW040739250326
834688LV00031B/362